What Remains

What Remains

The Many Ways We Say Goodbye
An Anthology

Sandi Gelles-Cole and Kenneth Salzmann, editors

Published by Gelles-Cole Literary Enterprises
www.LiteraryEnterprises.com

ISBN 978-1-7335885-0-8

Cover and interior formatting by Lawrence Matez (lmatez.com)
Cover photo by Kenneth Salzmann

Printed in the United States of America.

Love is stronger than death.

—SG-C

You only truly die when your name is spoken for the last time.

--Anonymous

Table of Contents

Foreword

We knew two things upfront, when we decided to compile an anthology exploring contemporary practices and rituals around funerals and memorials.

First, it was clear that many people were upending tradition when it came to memorializing a loved one—or planning for their own demise.

We had seen the occasional newspaper article about people taking personalized funeral rituals to the extreme. The Ohio man who rode off to eternity astride his beloved 1967 Harley-Davidson Electra Glide motorcycle, encased in an oversized plexiglass casket. The young boxer in Puerto Rico dressed for the ring and propped upright against the ropes at his wake. China's attempts to crack down on the popular if controversial practice of hiring strippers to perform at funerals, a practice designed to ensure a full house of mourners.

We had also seen the occasional pull-out-the-stops obituary gone viral, like that of the Tennessee man whose obit was pegged—with a dose of humor and without apology—to his one-time theft of a chained-up dog. Or that of the lifelong prankster in Connecticut whose lengthy obituary was a loving if irreverent catalogue of the departed 82-year-old's good-natured outrages and practical jokes over the course of "a lifetime of frugality, hoarding and cheap mischief, often at the expense of others."

Similarly, we had seen that, characteristically, our own generation—the ubiquitous Baby Boom—was putting its own distinctive mark on life's final passage, much as it had done all along the way. Who could be surprised that this fresh take on memorializing a loved one (or oneself) runs the gamut from the global popularity of "Death Cafes" turning a once-taboo topic into probing group discussions to personally crafting a coffin for a loved one, or oneself? Or by such emerging practices as pressing ashes into a vinyl record or incorporating them into a windchime to radical new strategies for laying someone to rest, such as a "mushroom death suit" like the one the late actor Luke Perry was buried in?

Developed by Jae Rhim Lee, an M.I.T. research fellow, the cotton jumpsuit covered with mushroom spores filters out toxins in the decomposing body at the same time it assists in decomposition. But the mushroom suit is only one of numerous emerging "green" solutions to funeral practices that can harm the environment. In Washington State, human composting—or recomposition—was recently legalized to offer an environmentally sound alternative to traditional burial or cremation.

But we also knew that there are quieter trends, just as radical in their own way, transforming the way we encounter death in contemporary culture—and that the writers and poets who answered our call for submissions would be the people who, in the final analysis, determined just what *What Remains* would be about and to whom it would speak. So instead of funerals bordering on carnival acts, look to *What Remains* for nuanced, often surprising writing about how we mark that final passage.

Who are the writers? They're acclaimed veterans of the literary world and, in a few cases, first-time authors. They're accomplished writers and poets with compelling stories to share. They live in Indonesia and in Ireland, France, Canada, and Mexico. Hawaii and New England and nearly everywhere in between. Collectively, they have written dozens of books, their work has been featured in dozens of anthologies, won numerous awards, earned them prestigious fellowships, been heard on *The Writer's Almanac*, and populated the pages of hundreds of newspapers, literary journals, and magazines, including: *The New York Times* and the *Daily News*; *The SUN*; *Poetry*; *Paris Review*; *TriQuarterly*; *Salon Magazine*; *Rattle*; *Women's Studies Quarterly*; *The Literary Journal of the Kurt Vonnegut Museum and Library*; *The Harvard Advocate*; *Poetry of Resistance: Voices for Social Justice* (University of Arizona Press); *Visiting Frost: Poems Inspired by the Life and Work of Robert Frost* (The University of Iowa Press); *Inside HigherEd*; *Calyx*; *Writer's Digest*; and many, many more.

As it turns out, not one of them wrote about burying an 82-year-old atop a Harley, but we're pretty sure they found their way to deeper truths that will resonate with readers.

--The Editors

♦ ♦ ♦

Virginia Barrett

RUB SALT IN HER MOUTH

A girl nearing three years old comes out of the house and leans on Ambuya's knee.

"You know her, yes?" Ambuya asks me.

When I look unsure, she tells me, "But you saved her life VeeGee. This is Blessing."

"Blessing!" I say, surprised to find her so changed: a strong-bodied little girl now, although still shy, I see. Blessing is the daughter of Ambuya's grandniece, Ruth, a young woman in her early twenties. Blessing's father was killed in a freak bus accident when I lived at the house two years ago, run over by another driver who was backing up his bus.

Some blamed *ngozi*, a bad spirit, which had attached itself to the owner of the company, the one driving the fatal bus. Ruth had not been given any widow dues—or insurance payment we'd call it—by the time I left Zimbabwe in 2002, because if the accident were determined to be the act of *ngozi*, then the owner was not personally responsible. This is what was explained to me; I never learned who exactly was in charge of determining liability.

I attended the wake with my host mother Ambuya, held at the compound of the deceased man's parents. I sat on the floor, legs stretched out with the other women in a hot, small room as the men continuously drummed outside for their dead relative. At one point, his grieving grandmother stumbled into the room, moaning loudly, and then, as if possessed, swooned to the floor near our feet, her body shuddering violently as she seemingly fell unconscious.

Two of the seven women gathered there lunged toward her, laying their hands on her body, while another woman leapt up and started pawing through her handbag until she extracted some house keys.

These she placed in the grandmother's trembling hand and held them there by folding her own hands over the old woman's. Then another woman rubbed salt in the grandmother's mouth, extracted from a jar left in the corner of the room.

Ambuya later told me that the metal of the keys grounded the grandmother to the earth so the bad spirits, trying to possess her at a vulnerable time of intense grief, would be thwarted; the salt also drove any possible *ngozi* out of her body. While the energy in the room was hauntingly urgent, to me the behavior of the grandmother seemed expected, too. After all, the women present had known immediately how to react.

I had never attended any kind of wake before, and the only funerals I had been to were for my paternal grandparents: sedate Anglo gatherings to say the least. The grandmother's intense, outward behavior provided a release for her I decided, within a supportive environment, like Ruth's loud wailing I sometimes heard coming from her room for weeks after the accident.

Soon after the death of her father, little Blessing fell sick with intestinal worms and thrush. They showed me one of the worms the clinic found in her excrement: deathly white and so long I couldn't believe it came out of a little child. Ruth asked me in a humble tone mixed with deep anxiety, if I could buy the prescribed medicine for Blessing, which I more than willingly did. I believe it cost under seven dollars. Thankfully, it cleared up the problem and the family claimed that I had saved her life, although I know Ambuya would have readily bought the medicine, too—dear blessings on us all.

Virginia Barrett

DEATH OF A GRANDSON: ZIMBABWE

> *Rub salt in her mouth—drive bad spirits out.*
> *Hold keys in her hand,*
> *and she will rise up again, for Blessing, fatherless child.*
>
> *--Ndiri Kuwira (I am Falling Down)*

Even the mourning dove
calls with a syncopated sound;
like a mourning dove—
how does a family grieve their love?
Drums: through the township they resound.
For three days steady rhythms pound
into the morning. *My dove.*

Sidney Bending

SIBLINGS

Born 9 years apart.
Died 9 years apart.

I keep their ashes
9 yards apart.

Hannah Bleier

CONSTANTS AT MEMORIALS

Someone waits too long to take the baby out.
While the bereaved try to choke
out a few words, the undaunted child shouts
gibberish, learning to talk *right now*.
We're angry at her, guilty for our anger.
Words spoken, while pretty or moving,
pale when compared with words unspoken.
What did the son mean by, "could be difficult?"
Why was "charming" said a dozen times,
but "kind" or "loving," never?
Heavy food before or after,
a visit with a friend.
Twenty years have passed.
"Your face looks the same, except
no red lipstick. You were so vivid."
"It's in my bag," I say. "Ruby Flame."
She shakes her dyed-blonde head.
"I love the names." We have our small ways
of skirting Death's approach. At services we nod
to him, slouched in the corner in his folding chair.

Nancy Brewka-Clark

FAMILY PLOT

Buying a coffin's easier than it sounds.
After all, it isn't as if we have to live with it.
The mortician's young enough to be our son.
Our ties go deep. His grandfather buried
our grandparents. His father buried our dad.
Somber at the start of the negotiations,
he eventually sees we're stable, not going
to go to pieces, not going to do much
but sit there dry-eyed, two married sisters
over fifty, over any vestigial fear
of being orphaned. Eventually the three of us
descend into the showroom where he's parked
a lot of caskets bumper to bumper. He steers
the two of us to a Rolls Royce, snow white
with an enameled plaque of violets
bunched around a calligraphic "Mother"
on the lid. We admire the quilted satin,
brass handrails, bulletproof liner,
but buy a modest Ford the sheen
and tint of a mourning dove. Above ground,
starting to fill out the paperwork, he says,
"Gosh, ladies, I think I left the light on
down there. Do me a favor and shut it off?
The switch is at the bottom of the stairs."
When only one of us moves to stand up,
he shakes his head. "Don't go alone."
Back down we go, quietly sharing a laugh.
Does he really think empty coffins

would scare us to death? Then it dawns on us
what he hopes we'll do: pick out another two.

Laurie Byro

SOUTHEAST LIGHTHOUSE STAIRS, BLOCK ISLAND

From the north the winds lie long and light slants
differently this time. I stick October into a socket of bone,
readjust its broken arm. I howl beside the goldenrod

along these cliffs, startle finches into flight. Ragged
feather dusters of cattails rove between their shoulders.

The air is yellowed with dust. I carry all of her there, a mosaic
of stones and fragments of bones, a skeleton key
with no door to open. She is the lazy strain of lost shells,

the deep green and copper rust of the body. Climbing
down nine flights of stairs, sometimes chasing the light

I lay her down among the tall grass. She is the flinty spark
off a match I cannot strike. A gingham dog tears at my father's
hand, laps his last slurp of water. I lie to the man who wants her

ashes to mingle with his. I tell him I have saved all of her
for him. I want the sea to take back all of my mistakes. Carved

and thick as a pane of old glass the tide sweeps
the beach. It picks through stones with crooked fingers of salt.
The tide, they tell me, will be coming in soon.

Dane Cervine

THE SOUND

It is 3:30 in the morning when we arrive at Wild Dove Lane just outside of Mariposa, a small town in the California mountains near Yosemite. The moon is luminescent as we wind slowly up the dusty clay road to my parents' property, and the scattering of small redwood hexagons my father fashioned into a home. He calls the hexagons, pentagon, work shed, and glass hexagonal meditation chamber *The Village of Shangri-La* from his favorite childhood book. My children lie asleep in the van, my wife rouses, asks how I'm doing. My father has just died, and I can only say *we are here*.

Opening the van door, Tashi—half wolf, half Malamute Husky—whimpers & wriggles as he always does when we come. In the dark, I can make out a huddled group of women sitting on the deck of the Jade House, a small two-story hexagon. They rise from the tables my father, Del, had built—cedar rounds perched on logs with black hexagonal tabletops trimmed in green. My mother, Bonnie, is among them—harbored by this group of women friends. We embrace, grateful to be together under this moon, to face this particular night.

We walk to where my father died on the Pagoda Hex, the half-finished structure my parents were hoping to move into someday. Carefully, we climb the makeshift wooden ladder to the second story where Del had fallen to a heart attack earlier in the day. My mom points out the white plastic chair with the faded blue cushion he must have been sitting in when it happened. How it must have toppled over, Del falling to the

24

floor as his heart stopped. I sit down in the same chair, now righted—listen to her tell the story...

How she left early that morning for town to open Synchronicity, her metaphysical book & gift store. How she was gone well into the evening, returning about 9:30pm, but didn't see Del in his chair in the First Hex where he would usually be: dozing, listening to music, watching a movie. How she looked for him past the Jade House, past Tea House II, the Magic Hex, the large House of Serenity—knowing as she climbed the Pagoda Hex stairs that he might be there, that something might have happened. It was peaceful, the white light of pin-point stars overhead, the luminous moon, the brush of wind, its sound in the treetops always like the sea. Del was lying on his back still in his work-boots and kneepads, eyes closed, mouth relaxed. He was cold, his body stiff.

Bonnie knew he must have been there since earlier in the day, how he liked to slowly work, then meditate—moving back and forth between the two till it was time for something cold to drink, something to eat. She knelt next to him, wept, offered up a prayer. Then the calls went out, for women friends to come quickly, for her children to come as soon as they could.

I'd known I would not see him on the Pagoda Hex when I arrived. Mom had called my cell phone, told me the Sheriff-Coroner had come, was preparing to take the body away, was willing to wait a little while but not as long as it would take for us to get there. That once the coroner's body bag was zipped shut, by law it couldn't be opened again till the autopsy. That anyone who died without having had a recent doctor's visit must have an autopsy. We joked later with mom that it might also have had something to do with the queer scene the young sheriff entered that night, the long snaking drive up the dirt road in the middle of night, the strange village of hexagons dimly lit by the yellow light of Japanese paper lanterns, the "coven" of women huddled round the prone body on the top of a rickety second-floor hex, chanting and howling at the moon with the huge wolf-dog. *Was this a deranged cult of women who sacrifice husbands in the middle of the forest?* Or was this just what it was: another death, another night.

The next morning, I wander into the First Hex, ease into his chair while my mom recounts the story to others on the phone. My mind is peaceful, relaxed. I look around the room, notice my father's dark hat, his olive-green jacket. Suddenly, I am overwhelmed with a sense of his presence, as though an orb-of-being much larger than I literally sits down in the chair with me, through me. I begin a sweet, compelling cry. A series of sensations, symbols, meanings move rapidly through my mind in a kind of *synesthesia*, my senses merging with the objects around me like a dream:

I see the white paper lantern over my mom's chair, with two black Japanese characters facing each other, one looking like a person reaching out to a troubled mass of lines adjacent. My father is here, reaching towards me, insistent. Then the jade colored Kleenex box with peach-colored flowers and a bright red hummingbird glowing on the stand next to me—this, he tells me, is his life now, more vibrant, varied, and beautiful than ever. Next, his dark brown walking hat and dusty jacket on the wall suddenly hang jauntily on a figure that, in my mind's eye, looks more like my dad than he had ever looked himself. He winks at me down an autumn colored path while James Taylor's "October Road" plays— songs from this album had been playing all month in my car, at home, in my mind when I woke and fell asleep. My father is impressing on me that these colors, the rich orange, brown and green of the album's cover, are his colors now—that his life has grown so much larger already, hatched from the sweet egg of human life. That he will always be with me. That we will talk again.

His presence gently lifts. I am shattered, yet so happy in this grief. Somehow, some part of him has connected with some part of me that will shape how I experience death, life, and the infinite shades between. As a therapist, I know enough to watch this avoidance of death in me with a careful eye. My existential heart understands death's finality. My mystical bones lean into the larger mystery.

Wandering outside, standing an inch away from the body-length chimes Del hung outside Teahouse II, I let the *Om* of deep sound resonate through my chest as the wind plays each bell. I hum into this tone: both *fatherless & fatherful.*

♦ ♦ ♦

Dane Cervine

THE MOLECULES OF THE DEAD

The Chapel of Light lies on Belmont Avenue in Fresno, across from a sprawling graveyard lined with palm and pine trees. Headstones nestle in the grass, mortal markers of the body's last resting place. Thousands, molecule by molecule, lose their familiar shape of torso, crook of arm, splay of hair—melt into root and mulch. My father has died, but will not join them. He will be cremated in the Chapel of Light.

We arrive in caravan—two cars of siblings, mother—for a viewing of my father's body before he is turned to ash. Pausing before the sign *Everything In One Beautiful Place*, we chuckle wryly—look round to see if by mistake we've stumbled upon a bad B-movie set.

The double doors open, reveal the funeral home director, middle-age face scarred by old pimples, the dour black suit. We learn the viewing room is not yet ready, so wander down the corridors of the vaulted building. I pick up a tan flyer announcing 25% off all mausoleum crypts and niches. The ceilings are high, the walls ornate—fountains of stone and water nestle at the end of each corridor, soft music wafting down endless hallways.

I touch the cold marble crypts, gold embossed names, dates. Layer upon layer of loved ones embalmed in elaborate polished wood caskets lined with white silk, blue velvet—so austere a resting place for skin, bone—bodies turning to dust in suit and tie, or pearls. I am drawn more to the brass urns, sitting row upon row in their niches, in the shapes of books, vases, clocks.

I'd prefer to be a book, have always wanted to be a book. But not stacked on a shelf like this; rather, opened and emptied, the ashes of every page fluttering into wind that must hold an infinite number of molecules of the dead.

I sit down at the end of one particularly beautiful room— light through the window just so, sound of falling water, lilt of flute, comfortable leather chair as I contemplate the rows of urns. And then, I feel him. A wisp of my father's presence—quiet, a hush of air, a brushing of the ethers— something tender, resonant, jovial. It is tangible, but brief.

Then it is time. My family gathers then walks down a long corridor till we stop just outside the viewing room. The funeral director pauses, explains what we'll see when we enter the room so we'll know what to expect.

I think we unsettled the Neptune Society connected with the chapel, the organization responsible for collecting and cremating the body. They were expecting to deliver the urn, that's all. But we wanted to see him again—father, husband— before turning him to ash. They agreed, but there would be no casket, no makeup. He would be in a large cardboard box, under a shawl. We smile at this, think it fitting for my father's sense of humor.

And now, here he is, lying so still beneath his blue shawl in his cardboard box. White trimmed beard soft—but skin cold, chilled from the freezer he has been in. We cry, make farewells, hold his hand, stroke his face, his broad stiff chest, tell stories. My brother dances a sailor's jig, having promised dad he'd do so. And we sing: a favorite song from the movie South Pacific called *Bali High,* then an old church hymn. Finally, it is time to go.

We leave him there, in the Chapel of Light—the last time we'll ever see him. Until the drive back, up the dirt road into his forest, and I see the redwood-roofed hexagons he had built as home, as monument to his way of being in the world. He is everywhere—in shivered wood planks cut by his own hand, in Japanese lantern and Shoji-screened doors crafted in his workshop, hammered deep into memory, into bone.

Holding onto each other in a tight circle beneath the crescent moon—my father somehow in the middle of it all—we know we indeed have *everything in one beautiful place*...the molecules of the dead and the living mixing together, here, inside.

◆ ◆ ◆

Lucia Cherciu

THE SOUL WAS THIRSTY

They paid a woman to water my father's grave
for forty days. She filled two buckets,

walked to the cemetery every morning,
and lit candles at the grave. She didn't know

my father, so she just looked at the picture,
crossed herself, checked off on her list. The soul

was thirsty and needed some water to wait out
the time before ascent. Roses had already started

to open and some teenagers came in and picked them
to sell at the farmers' market. Defiant, the flowers

fought for space. Uneasy, the woman
was afraid to confront the petty thieves

even when they stole the wrought iron bars
of the fence to sell for scrap metal.

Marc Alan Di Martino

REQUIEM FOR AN OCEAN BURIAL

You wanted a rocky shoreline off the coast of Maine
with barbarous waves, a few small fishing boats,
a lighthouse reaching out across the fog
like a tired hand, waving farewell forever.

What you got was a cramped room in a nursing home
which cost a fortune and drained your bank account,
three drab meals a day, reruns of *Seinfeld,*
bingo on Sunday. And you don't even play.

When I think of you now I see my daughter
wheeling you through the East Asian wing
of the Virginia Museum of Fine Arts, pointing
to paintings of cherry blossoms, inviting comment

as you stare at the walls, the delicate pink flowers
on their silk beds confounding you. *How did we get here?*
I wonder - but I know well how you burned
three marriages and plunged headfirst down the stairs

in a gambit for unrequited love. Me,
I'm sick of losing people. My whole life I've been
a tree, my leaves peeling off, standing there
in the storm, waiting it out. You're still alive, of course,

but no telescope on earth is powerful enough
to reach you. Television fills the cracks of your life
the way your children once did, exactly the way

your grandchildren should. But your mind has gone

for a stroll someplace - a better place than this.
You no longer know who the president is
and I envy you that, the involuntary bliss
of your ignorance; you're spared the rituals

of self-immolation the nation endures
in your absence, though you still recall the day
JFK was shot - each stark detail of your day -
while we have *Where were you when you got the results*

and how many weeks did you cry? You'll never know
what it did to us, how it wedged us apart, turned us
into a Civil War family, Union vs. Confederate
contending it out until there was nothing left

to argue over but a fifty-thousand dollar
insurance policy in your name signed *Luv,*
Mom. Heirs to pettiness. Still, I picture you
clipping coupons at the kitchen counter

Saturday mornings - that was how you took
your mind off things. Your whole life has amounted
to saving cents even as you lost yours. Bare ruined choirs
sing to you now in your blistering senescence.

Here the narrative   breaks
                                        down.   All
                                              the king's
                                                    men
can't put you back together   again.

                                The ocean
calls to you, its patient uterus   throbbing
with motherly love   as we arrange
                                        for
                                your ashes
                to be scattered over the kicking waves.

                        א

        You'll never know that to your final breath
        you were my first and every troubled thought.

J. C. Elkin

IN MEMORIUM

Philip Roth said, *"What cemeteries prove, at least to people like me, is not that the dead are present but that they are gone."* That much was obvious the first time I saw my mother's gravestone four months after her funeral. If she were there, she would have opened a sink hole that sucked it down to Hell.

She had been so clear in planning her funeral, the only aspect of brain cancer she could control, and this was not what she ordered. My father, in his widower's desperation, had forgotten her final directives from that drizzly February day at the monument shop on the edge of town when Mom, like Scrooge at his own burial, had prepared hers.

The claustrophobic showroom was dingy and silent, save for my parents' murmurs as they flipped through catalogs of statuary, markers, and sarcophagi. My brother and I, children in their memory only, milled around for what seemed an eternity, waiting for service.

"They must be really busy in back," he whispered, motioning outside to an angel Gabriel standing vigil over a snowy plot of granite slabs. "People are just dying to get in here."

I snorted, struggling to contain forty years of giggles. It was Mom's one sure-fire joke, which she'd told every time we passed the cemetery for as long as I could remember.

A matronly woman in soft shoes materialized from the back room and Mom, in her clear, teacher voice, explained precisely what she wanted: a modest and dark double headstone. *No pink granite, no carved flowers, no hearts or cherubs.*

Nothing to attract attention, she said. Once they settled on a modest charcoal grey, the saleswoman flipped open a metal clipboard of invoice forms, and asked my mother to spell her name.

Only then, when she began dictating her epitaph, did she break down sobbing, her momentary grief eclipsing her sunny outlook like a cloudburst. Ever since receiving her diagnosis two months earlier, all she had talked about was how she couldn't wait to get to heaven. My father held her to his broad chest as she blubbered incoherently into her embroidered hanky, and we kids stood at her side as useless as our unspoken words.

The stone she wanted was on backorder, so we left a deposit and went home. There she laid out her interment clothes for me, explaining all the specifics: a gold crucifix and the vestments of her lay vocation—Third Order Dominicans—including a white pinafore and scapular she stressed as being most important. "I don't trust your father to remember," she said pointedly.

She might have said the same about me. For when the time came a month later, though I sent the correct garments to the funeral home, I panicked last minute that I'd included my panties, neatly folded inside, instead of hers. We were not nearly the same size, and I pictured her walking around Heaven sans underwear, cursing me.

When I confessed to her friend, she said, "Lois would be laughing her head off," and I realized she was right. Mom didn't do *somber,* which may explain our later behavior.

Folks said to my brother, *I'm sorry about your mother,* and he shrugged, "Nah – you didn't do it."

My father kept repeating, "I just wish it had been me, instead," to which I unthinkingly replied, "We all feel that way."

My uncle led a small chorus of singers, including my teenaged daughters, in *The Hoco Moco Isle*, a silly Vaudeville number that had served as lullaby to three generations.

Mom would have loved that, but she would have hated her grave when the marker was finally in place. My father had accepted a pink stone when the grey model Mom ordered kept getting delayed. All I knew was that it was "bigger and nicer" and that he'd gotten "a great deal." Not only was it pink, but it was bigger than she wanted with pedestals for flowers. No one in our family ever brought flowers to a gravesite, but perhaps he planned to start. "Bring them to me while I'm alive," Mom used to say. If she were still there, though, she would appreciate the lilacs that bloomed every year for Memorial Day.

Standing awkwardly at her grave, I apologized out loud on my father's behalf, feeling stupid for talking to no one. Mom had moved on, probably forgotten she ever cared about her headstone. Besides, what could I do now? Send it back?

Well, maybe. Someday.

♦♦♦

Meredith Escudier

JOSETTE'S FUNERAL

For most people, attending a memorial service is not a match made in heaven. Still, when our presence is solicited, we respond to the call. It is the understandable mark of respect that we, the living, can and must provide—to the departed, to the entourage and to ourselves as fellow members of humanity. So, when our neighbor in the south of France died, attending Josette's funeral was the least we could offer: Show our faces, mark our support and join the ranks. No originality required.

I play my part sincerely and discreetly, giving a nod here, linking an arm there. Ten years in the village have given our Franco-American couple, if not insider status, a respectable place for positive participation. And I will miss Josette, not because of a true intimacy we shared, but as the friendly, knowledgeable neighbor she was, a person who drew much of her prestige (and information) from her stint as café owner and server of countless *cafés* and *pastis*.

Would I come back to the house for a sip of soda afterwards? A Perrier perhaps? Somehow, the bereft family had granted me special status as the next-door neighbor. I hesitated, not wanting to intrude…well, just for a minute. But *quelle minute*. That's when I encountered Josette's 20-something granddaughter, Elodie, in all of her unembarrassed youth. Admittedly, Elodie and I were not meant to meet, and the generational and cultural divide didn't help much either. Moreover, religion can be a divisive subject. Touchy even. And oh yes, so is death. Still, I had trouble processing what was about to come. Just as I made ready to go, Elodie rushed over to me in all of her unbridled lust for life.

"Will you say hello to my grandmother when you see her?"

Huh?

Her eyes shone brightly, counting on me to transmit her advance greetings to her grandmother (in heaven?) and clearly, it would be convenient for her if I could manage this sooner than later.

Stunned, *sans* repartee, I stopped dead in my tracks. For one thing, I was not feeling particularly decrepit that day. Yes, I was a good 30 years older than Elodie, which placed me squarely into the category of all Old People (over 30). However, I had been feeling sort of sprightly up until that moment and although the mirror reflected a face that was – shall we say? – *inhabited,* my mascara had been applied with a steady hand and I'm quite sure my lipstick had missed my teeth that day.

Elodie remained unperturbed…and expectant. Well, would I or wouldn't I? Still stupefied, I looked into her face, so unmapped by life's peregrinations, bursting with the glow of self-confidence. *Elodie, dear…*but where to begin? Instead, I chose the easy way out. I nodded a vague *oui* to her request and inched my way to the door, now burdened by the oddest promise to the next generation and saddled with a volunteer activity not of my choosing.

What was I thinking? Was it for the living? The dead? The awkward, surreal, grandiose foolishness of life? I'm not sure, but maybe it was somehow just for Josette.

◆◆◆

Beverly Butler Faragasso

FINAL PROGRAM

I am not looking for them, these funeral programs. Random papers thrown into drawers are my targets this day of spring cleaning, so when I find the programs, I am surprised. I did not remember I had them. The programs belonged to my parents and I must have gathered them up during that awful last day in their house before the moving van took away all their furniture and all their clothes, indeed all their possessions.

I am sitting on the floor in my dining room, the place where my parents would have stored these programs in their own house. The still faces captured in black and white and chosen, I assume, by a family member for the front panel intrigue me. When I was younger, I never understood why my parents didn't toss these programs into the trash once the funerals were over. It was morbid, I declared, in my youthful arrogance.

I find the program for my maternal grandmother, who lived in my parents' home from the time I was two until her death eighteen years later. She seemed to be surprised and pre-occupied as her picture was being taken, her mind probably focused on turning a hem or icing a cake. I still have one of her hand-stitched quilts. There are a few holes in it and some of the batting has popped out, but I love to run my fingers over the three-dimensional rise of her stitches and knots. The delicious smell of her fresh-baked coconut cake often wafted into the bedroom I shared with my sister, and I wish I could have a slice now.

I open the program and I am struck by the simplicity of my grandmother's life. She lived for family and church. I imagine I can see her shoes, sturdy, no-nonsense, laced up, meant for purposeful walking and standing. Now, suddenly, I am walking with her and my mother to my Saturday art class. I am about nine or ten. Then, as quickly, for reasons I cannot explain, my eye focusses on the date of her death and I feel an old regret that she died the semester *before* I received my bachelor's degree. *Just* one semester, *just* one degree of separation between her death and the beginning of my life as an independent adult. In the years since, I have often wondered what this woman from rural South Carolina whose life revolved around family and church would think of her granddaughter's life: would she think I was too busy, trying to do too much? In the end, I decide that she would have been proud that I had a good job, I traveled the world and I waited until I was fifty-one to marry the right man for me. Yes, I think she would have been proud.

I am glad I read her program first. Having her quilt is wonderful. Remembering the smell and taste of her cake is phenomenal. But, holding my grandmother's entire life in my hands in the form of a folded four-panel program, however, has been more precious than words or possessions. I walked again with my grandmother! Because of that, I pick up the next program and the next and the next and the next and I sit quietly in the lives of those who came before me. My parents were wise to keep all these mementos to the dead. They understood the emotional and transformative power of the printed page, and I am grateful, *at last.*

◆ ◆ ◆

Jeanne Finley

THE HORSE THAT EVIL BUILT

What goes around comes around.
— Common saying

Since October 6, 2018, the day of the catastrophe, spring and early summer have been kind: the limousine's deep wheel gashes have been filled in somewhat by overgrowth, and greening has softened the upstate countryside around the parking lot of the popular Apple Barrel Country Store and Cafe in Schoharie County. A tributary of the Schoharie Creek is little more than a drainage ditch here at the bottom of the gully, and a white wooden cross on its bank is like a stalwart young tree that has erupted since last year's leaves fell.

Now it is July, and in the parking lot, the memorial itself is made of common wood, a simple sawhorse with twenty small rough-hewn wooden crosses nailed to its crossbar for each of the innocents who were killed that day: seventeen passengers in the limousine, the driver, and two bystanders who had just finished lunch and were talking outside. The sawhorse suggests an earlier police barricade down to the ravine and creek, where the limousine finally stopped. A string of Christmas lights is woven between the crosses, and atop the crossbar are small bags of offerings, contents unknown, as well as pens for mourners to write messages. Spread out on the ground are bouquets of artificial flowers, photographs, rosaries, angel wings, flags, personal talismans of grief. Dozens of short messages cover the sawhorse, top to bottom, some printed in Magic Marker, some incised in the soft wood, all addressed directly to the individuals who died there. "Savannah I want you back!!! Dad" is one. But the writing is fading, victim of three seasons outdoors. Another memorial—a formal, less raw, more forward-looking plan of steppingstones and trees—is in the works, if enough funds can be found.

The 2001 Ford Excursion stretch limousine, modified and elongated to carry nearly double the number of passengers that safety regulations allowed, came roaring down the hill of Route 30A in the middle of that October Saturday. It blew through the stop sign at the Route 30 T-intersection (there were no skid marks anywhere) and kept going, narrowly missing a car; kept going into the Apple Barrel's parking lot, kept going into a parked SUV, which then hit and threw the two bystanders, kept going down the incline into the ravine and the creek, where its irresistible force was finally stopped by the earthen banks and the sumac trees just turning scarlet and the impact that the hurtling four-ton weapon of mass destruction had on those immovable elements. Catastrophic brake failure, said a prosecution consultant's report, which should have exonerated the driver, although toxicology tests showed he had a significant level of marijuana in his system. One of the twenty crosses is covered with a black cloth. He's there, among the dead, but nobody wants to acknowledge him. I find this saddest of all.

The passengers were young, ages 24 to 34, among them four sisters, their three husbands, two recently married couples, and one husband's brother. October 6 was Amy Steenberg's 30th birthday. On her gravestone dates, the month and day are the same. Most were from Amsterdam, an old mill city on the Mohawk River's Rust Belt. They were all going to a birthday party Amy's husband Axel had organized in Cooperstown at a brewery. They wanted to do the right thing, drink but not drive, so they hired a bus, which didn't show up. Anxious that they wouldn't reach the brewery in time for their reservation, one of them began to cold-call car services, finally reaching Prestige Limousines in Wilton, New York, managed by Nauman Hussain, the son of the owner, Shahed Hussain, a Pakistani businessman with a history of fraud and bankruptcies. "There's nothing that he would touch that you would trust," said a lawyer who'd seen Shahed in action. "If he fixed your elevator, take the stairs." This does not indict Pakistanis or immigrants or Muslims, unless you believe in the naïve fallacy of inductive logic, that one individual can indict a whole ethnicity, religion, category. No, the links in the chain are much more linear than that.

Nauman, the owner's son, was young and the limo was available; the driver was not young but he was available; the limo and Shahed, its owner, were not young, but Shahed was not available, having gone back to Pakistan in March, immigration in reverse. Nauman, you see, managed operations for his father *in absentia*, but his father owned the company, along with a rundown motel. Shahed's name, not Nauman's, is on the incorporation papers, on the bank accounts, the deeds, the titles, the court filings, the inspection reports: SHAHED MALIK HUSSAIN, OWNER. Yet he has borne no ownerly consequences to date. Nor has a legal indictment of Shahed come, it will never come, since no one, incomprehensibly enough, has asked him to return to the U.S. for questioning, nor has he been extradited, although Nauman has been charged with twenty counts of criminally negligent homicide. The trial is set for January 2020.

But how did we get to this point? If we reverse the long, terrible slide of the limousine into oblivion by stating the facts and the links back through time, a "House That Jack Built" cause and effect, it's possible to see how the rough wooden sawhorse has come to interpret the lives and deaths of twenty people:

These were the brakes that failed at the top of the hill.

These were the companies that inspected and passed the brakes, twice.

This was the vehicle whose safety inspections the State of New York repeatedly failed but failed to take off the road.

This is the father who let the son do whatever he wanted (or didn't want) in running the businesses, and left when the going got tough.

This is the man, Shahed Hussain, who informed for the FBI, and in his illustrious nine-year career put away seven men from Albany, Newburgh, and Pittsburgh. More innocents. Not terrorists. A snitch in the Muslims' house.

This is the money he got from the FBI that he used to buy limousines and a motel. And why did he work for the FBI?

This was his scheme in 2001, the year of the Ford Excursion: he solicited bribes from immigrants who didn't speak English to take their written driver license tests for them.

This was his punishment: deportation or prison. But the FBI said, there's another way. He can work for us, do whatever we want, just let him stay.

This was the offer, this was the choice, and they made his choice for him, and us, including the dead.

And this is the man who, before he stayed, was wanted for murder at home, but he came just the same because . . .

no one said hey, or wait, or stop,
no one said yes, no one said no,
no one said anything, ever, at all,

45

and no one's said anything up to this day.

So what do we make of the irony of an accused murderer and convicted felon who successfully scammed the Department of Motor Vehicles by procuring phony driver's licenses, and who is now ultimately responsible (though uncharged) for an unsafe vehicle that killed twenty people? There is no mention of any of this on the sawhorse in the parking lot, of course. Because

    this is the horse that evil built,
    and this is what happens
    when the brakes fail,
    when no one says stop,
    when no one says go,
    when someone says no
    when they should have said yes
    and when someone says yes
    when they should have said no.

◆ ◆ ◆

Nina Gaby

ON MENTIONING THAT OUR DAUGHTER WANTS TO BE A MORTICIAN

It happened again yesterday. I was sitting with our accountant, his fingers flying over the computer keys as he figured out our tax situation. I was staring at his profile as he stared at his screen. He had already asked the perfunctory, "So where is Zoe thinking of going to college next year?" undoubtedly more concerned with the "*How* will Zoe *afford* college next year" than the "*Where* is she going."

As I answered, I watched, in profile, the ever-so-slight raise to his eyebrow, the reflection of the computer screen in the widening eyes, the quick, almost imperceptible pursing of the lips. It is the reaction I have become accustomed to when I answered, "She's looking at a bachelor' s program in funeral administration. Undertaking."

The accountant is like most of the folks we know in our small town. They are nice, polite, and very cautious people. As small-town people they have learned to manage their reactions with care. That slight tension they seem to get around the lips as they process my response is quickly replaced with a bright smile. An ever-so-brief pause giving the synapses time to refire before saying, "Wow, she would be great at that!" or, "Well, she'll always have a job!"

Both those reactions bear exploration as we look ahead to our daughter's future. There is a serious side to our otherwise still silly teenager, a side that has struggled with anxiety and depression and loss. The anxiety and depression are part of our family legacy, that crap shoot of inherited brain chemistry. The loss piece, both real and anticipatory, is most

47

likely a direct result of being an only child born to older parents.

Because of this age differential, while her tiny cohorts were enjoying youthful grandparents and often still viable great-grandparents, she was dealing with bigger issues. Born after one grandfather already had died, she then witnessed a whole generation get buried in rapid succession, each relative within a few months of each other.

It was predictable that she would, early on, begin the conversation about the loss of us, her own parents. She often tried it out, it seemed testing the safety net, once tripping me on the hardwood stairs as I carried down a full laundry basket while wearing high heels. She was two, already psychologically mired in the glory days of magical thinking. Lurking, I am sure, under what seemed to be an innocent misinterpretation of cause and effect, was a real testing of what it might feel like to watch me not be there anymore.

To continue this discussion, no matter how difficult, and to soften this anticipation, I did what some might call a strange thing. My husband and I took Zoe with us to the memorial park in our hometown, where much of our family is buried, to look for plots while they were having their annual sale. We never wanted her to feel left alone with decisions to make or services to be paid for when the inevitable happened.

We chose a sunny Sunday. She was about four or five. We bought bunches of daisies for the graves of our family members and a big cherry pie for later from the farm stand across the road. As we drove around the park with the saleswoman, looking for the four plots we were planning to pre-buy, I asked the saleswoman to stop the car in the section we were considering. I got out, much as one might do when looking at real estate, and lay down in the grass under the tree at the head of one of the plots. Very deliberately I stayed there for a few moments as my husband, little girl, and the wide-eyed saleswoman stared out the car window. I told my husband later I was making a memory. My daughter will never be able to visit our graves without laughing.

The saleswoman said that absolutely no one has ever done that before, but she recovered and was thrilled to have sold the four plots. Why four? They were on sale and the shade was irresistible.

To satisfy my own need for some sense of continuity, I take pleasure in the idea that maybe I planted the seeds of her career that day. We usually have lost a lot of influence by the time our kids reach the decision-making point in high school. But then, of course, my daughter's own fearlessness has cultivated those seeds. She, on the other hand, attributes it all to "Stubby," a beaver who died at the mouth of the wooden bridge across the road from our house and was left to decompose until only a few shards of bone were left. For months she visited Stubby, daring herself to watch the slow decay. Somewhere in a lost plastic bag, we have the tiny remains of Stubby, buried, most likely, under a pile of old clothes in a closet.

But yes, back to the original considerations. Yes, my daughter will probably always have a job. Not a bad deal for the cost of four years of school.

Sometimes I take the time to explain all that to people as their faces soften and we talk a little more about Zoe's plans. That 'end of life' is sexy stuff nowadays? Some folks get that. To others I explain the support she is getting for her high school Senior Project; the local undertaker is her mentor and says her paper on the psychological defense mechanisms used by morticians is the best he's ever read on the subject. Her drama teacher who has struggled with illness and his own mortality, is the pre-plan subject of her project. He has generously articulated what it really means to be staring it all in the face.

I talk about our visit to the college outside of Boston where one of the directors spent the entire afternoon with us, showing us the labs and the embalming room, the tidy little packets of restoring wax, and the displays of coffins and urns, the objects of her craft to be. I talk about how inclusive the program is, with its business courses and psychology department, as well as its importance as a center for bereavement research. How 'cutting edge.' I say that the college is willing to work with us to make it affordable, like they already believe in her. I admit how odd this is. Only one person has not taken it in stride. An elderly neighbor, who, while stopping to chat in front of the dairy counter at the co-op one day screamed at me. "Does she know what she's getting in to? She's going to have to touch dead people!" It was my turn to smile politely and move on.

As our accountant and I finished our tasks, I knew he got it. After all, as the adage goes: the only things certain in life are death and taxes. We said that to each other and rolled our eyes. I wrote the check for the taxes and smiled at the irony.

Elaine Garrett

THE LAKE

I can't remember the tale
But hear his voice still, a well
of dark water, a prayer.

from "The Gift", Li-Young Lee

It is a late fall picnic in the black and white photograph, and they look almost like Lara and Zhivago, or maybe Taylor and Burton, an impossibly handsome couple in a turtleneck and corduroy embrace.

Ty was a civil engineer, father to six; my Aunt Bette (like Davis), a bank teller, de-facto mother to her father's household. Their complicated family situations precluded their marriage for a decade, and it wasn't until my own adulthood I learned they lived those unwed years together in my grandfather's Second Street house. Bette became "ChaCha", a nickname necessary to distinguish her from the same named ex-wife.

Ty had grown up in comfortable wealth, weekends and summers spent at the family retreat an hour north of Manhattan. Despite his widowed mother's increasing senility, she lived the warmer months alone at the eponymous Tyrrel Lake, which contained 250 wooded acres, a Sears built cottage, and a boathouse later filled with souvenirs of her world travels. The road to the property ended at the garage across the lake; groceries, furniture and anything that would float hauled across by boat. In 1976 Mrs. T. walked into the woods for the last time, and Ty and ChaCha moved to "The Lake", its upkeep now their full-time vocation.

51

An assortment of relatives and friends helped finish the road to the house. They were summers of silent canoe trips through the water lilies, and teenagers leapt into the lake from the boathouse roof, just clearing the antlers mounted below. Children knee deep in sawdust helped Uncle Ty stack firewood, and bottle rockets rigged from recently drained beers arced across the night sky.

Though the road was now complete, nature did not yield control. Each rainstorm meant powerlines ensnarled with vegetation, and every spring the Beaver Convention of Eastern New York built dams strong enough to wash out the furthest bend of road. New overnight visitors to The Lake might ask in the morning about the blood curdling screams, but the bobcats' lamentations remained the secrets of the woods.

It was early fall 1984, when Ty lost control of the backhoe on the embankment near the garage. He jumped free before it could turn over on him, but the fall broke his neck. ChaCha said she knew almost immediately something was wrong when the sounds across the lake ceased. Over the next few weeks, as she learned to drive the Jeep to town and adjusted to a sudden, solitary life, she'd go out the back porch and scream her grief across the Lake, the response only her own echoes, calling back to her.

ChaCha, her sister Terrie, and a couple friends took off at sunrise one cold morning in November. They spread the balloon out in the area next to the garage, the pilot heating the air inside until they rose into the sky. ChaCha brought along a cassette player, and the group listened to Nat King Cole as the balloon glided over the Lake. Ty's ashes drifted down to the water and trees in a layer of memory, forever binding him to the place he loved, the place that had claimed him.

ChaCha stayed a handful of years more. There were summer parties, and two weddings—including her own. Eventually the burdens of the Lake became more than just unceasing labor. She needed to unmoor and leave behind her restless reminiscence.

Many years later I inherited several boxes of ChaCha's photographs, though none, it seems, of the hot air balloon on that fall day. But there is one I have, now proof of memory lived: A Polaroid of the early morning sun, taken as the light glinted through the towering rhododendron, illuminating a floral cathedral on the edge of the forest.

◆ ◆ ◆

Sandi Gelles-Cole

THE EXECUTIONER

The vet came to our living room carrying the black doctor's bag which contained the sedative and the killing injection which he administered directly into my golden retriever's heart. Charley didn't die after the first lethal dose. I knew he was waiting for me to give him permission to pass over the rainbow bridge as I've heard animal people refer to their pet's passing.

"It's okay, boy, you can go now. It's time."

His head hit the couch pillow and he was gone, then carried away in a Mexican blanket by his dog walker to the crematorium. My husband had the misfortune to run into them on the street as they loaded the body into the car, and he saw Charley's lifeless head lolling about, no longer filled with whatever sweet doggie dreams and thoughts had occupied him for nearly 15 years.

He was my best friend, of course, and he had seen me through divorce, bankruptcy, surgery, sobriety, remarriage, professional highs and lows. He was my doppelganger. He was irreplaceable.

That is why I called the Animal Communicator. A professional therapist who will interpret what our pets are thinking whether they are alive or dead.

Go ahead and laugh. I certainly did when I first received promotional material from a communicator in Woodstock, but the day after Charley died I was in need and a friend I trusted had recommended a different expert. I had been prepared for Charley's passing. He was old and ill and as I was to learn from our post-death communication, hanging on only until he knew the family was ready.

Much came out of that phone session with the communicator. She apparently is a sensitive and picks up the dead's vibrations just as all mediums do. Charley revealed secrets about his other lives and what would happen now that this life was over. He called me his angel. I could not talk anymore and though I had time left on the session I never called back. I felt we had said goodbye.

A few months later I was ready to rescue another retriever. This dog, who I named Carlos in Charley's honor, had been thrown into the streets of Guadalajara.

I will not wait until Carlos dies to hear his story. Soon I will call the communicator to learn what he needs from us to heal. Most likely while we are on the phone I will be able to check in on Charley. His spirit is somewhere out there, and I am certain the animal communicator will locate him.

♦♦♦

Paul Hostovsky

NAUGHTON'S QUARTERS

Sometimes when I'm running
in the cemetery
I steal a few
quarters from Naughton

because I need them
for the parking meters
when I'm driving.
This I confide to a friend

over lunch, adding:
Naughton has plenty
and doesn't drive anymore anyway,
and it's not like Naughton's neighbors

notice. Plus his descendants
keep replenishing them--
it must be some kind of tradition,
like placing stones, or flowers--

and then there's the tradition
I'm upholding: the grave-
robber's tradition, the living taking from the dead
what the dead have no need of.

My friend stops chewing.
He looks alarmed, pillaged,

like he just bit down on something hard
and realized it was his own filling.

Put the quarters back, he says.
The dead have need. They have need.

Linda G. Kaplan

A MANTLE ON MY SHOULDERS

My mother was the main caregiver for my father who was in the final stages of Parkinson's disease. She was so deeply focused on trying to prevent placing him in a nursing home she ignored insistent signals from her own body. She had congestive heart failure and started dieting upon her doctor's advice, but she lost so much weight she could no longer eat.

Feeling that she wasn't getting any better, I changed doctors. When she attended the first visit, the new doctor immediately hospitalized her, whereupon it was discovered she had advanced colon cancer and immediate surgery was ordered. As she was waiting to be wheeled into the operating room, she thanked me for all I had done for her and told me she had no fear of death. My brother, who had flown in from Houston, arrived just as they were taking her from the room and the last words she spoke to him were "Don't fight with your sister!" I remind him of that fact often. She survived the surgery and was placed on a ventilator, after which she was no longer able to speak.

After a month still in the hospital on the ventilator, we were told that the cancer had metastasized into her lungs and there was no longer any hope. The family gathered around her bed as the doctor suspended the ventilator and she lay dying, unable to breathe on her own, gasping for breath. My brother, still unable to tell her she had cancer, stood at her feet yelling, "It was your heart, Mom!" Meanwhile, my nephew, a Head and Neck surgeon, stood behind me describing the process saying, "Her eyes are dilating. . . "

while I stood at her ear thanking her for all she had done for me, telling her to let go , that it was ok, and my sister in law and niece at her other ear whispering the same. Strangely, as her body was going through its process of shutting down, I felt a strange sense of lifting and a joy coming from her as her spirit left her shell-like body.

We are Jewish and in the Jewish tradition, out of respect, the body of the deceased is never left alone. Usually the undertaker provides someone to sit with the body, but there was a glitch and no one was immediately available. I offered to stay while my family went back home, and after nurses removed all the tubes from my mother's body, I entered her room.

As I sat in a chair close to the bed her body laid on, although I was alone, I felt a mantle being placed on my shoulders and intuitively felt it was a protection. My mother was never a touchy-feely woman. But denied that intimacy in life, I got to hold her hand for a long time in death, and to speak lovingly to her spirit. Finally, after many hours, someone from the funeral home came to relieve me and I went back home.

I came to learn later that it is considered a sacred honor in Judaism to attend the deceased, and only a person of great faith should be the one staying with the body. I have always loved G-d and have prayed every night since childhood, my faith so deep, it felt right that as my mother was there when I entered the world, I could be there for her as she departed. It truly was my greatest honor.

◆ ◆ ◆

Ronn Kilby

THEY FORGET THEY CAN FLY

I never knew Maria Valdez.

I only knew of her. Of the brave fight she put up the last few days of her very short life. But she was my first, so she always comes to mind.

The meeting room at Children's Hospital was plain, but for the flowers and the array of photos of three beautiful happy children. A favorite toy here, a framed report card there. A goodbye drawing from a younger sibling. As I set up to play, I was momentarily overcome, realizing the depth of the ocean of sorrow in which I had just immersed myself. My audience, after all, was composed of the people closest to little Maria Valdez, who didn't make it.

Something inside said, you can do nothing here. Leave now. But I didn't. I played. So it goes.

I spent my twenties performing in small clubs and bars on the east coast. Playing and singing for hippies and drunks and rich college girls. Good times. In some dives I actually *had* to dive to avoid the occasional beer bottle missile. I learned to read the crowd and adjust my song list accordingly.

But this was new territory. This was scary stuff. What the hell could I play for these people that wasn't patronizing or superficial? For some reason my fingers just naturally fell into "They Forget They Can Fly." As luck, providence, or serendipity would have it, this was a good choice. As I'll explain, directly.

So how and why did I end up playing this unlikely gig? The how is easy.

The why is more complicated. Guilt over a failed marriage left me seeking validation and meaning—through serial volunteering. My self-imposed penance included teaching adults to read, playing piano at the senior center, serving food at the homeless shelter, a jazz CD benefiting the Child Abuse Prevention Foundation. And of course—Children's Hospital.

And the song? Technically, it started in Africa. Or Ireland.

Nicky Arden was my very spiritual next-door neighbor. A South African native, she was the first white woman in her village to become a sangoma (medicine woman). That amazing journey is documented in her 1996 book, *African Spirits Speak.**

One evening, not long before that celebration for Maria, Nicky shared a story from her time in Africa. They had built a fence around their garden, to keep the goats out. Unfortunately, it did not keep the birds out—who quickly learned the veggies were quite tasty. They also had no fear of Nicky's rudimentary scarecrow - nor of Nicky. A gentle soul, she let them be, as there was plenty for all.

The curious thing was that they didn't fly away. Days later they were still hanging out in the garden. Actually walking around on the ground like pets. When she shooed them, they just ran. She said they had forgotten they could fly. Finally, one morning she came out and they were gone. Apparently they remembered.

That night her story of the birds became the stuff of my dreams. In which the birds became tiny angels who forgot they could fly, but eventually remembered. The next morning I picked up the guitar and wrote the piece. No words, more of a simple tone poem. One that ultimately resonated with the Children's audience. Why?

The technical answer is that it uses an open tuning (DADGAD) common to Celtic music. When strummed open, it sounds a Dsus4 chord—which is neither major nor minor. Neither happy nor sad. It shimmers. Combined with modal scales, and the sustained ringing of open notes, it has a haunting effect.

But there's a more abstract explanation as well. It also demands of the player a certain letting go. If you try to be too technically precise in fingering, you will fail. When you just let it happen, it's magical. You must not fight the guitar, you must let the guitar do the work. I think that "letting go" part resonates with the listener on a visceral level—especially a listener immersed in that ocean of sorrow.

I played many other pieces that night, some with a flautist friend joining in. And I played other nights for others grieving the loss of a child. Each time, I said *this is the last time.* Then I went again, one more time. And one more time. After nearly two years of more or less monthly engagement, I finally stopped. I had to move on. And, like the families, I had to let it go.

I never knew Maria Valdez. I only knew of her. I do know how humbled and honored I was to be part of that celebration of her life—and I know it was one I will never forget. I just hope she and her family remember they can fly.

◆ ◆ ◆

Scan the QR Code to hear "They Forget They Can Fly."

*You can find *African Spirits Speak* here:
www.amazon.com/African-Spirits-Speak-Journey-Tradition/dp/0892817526

♦ ♦ ♦

Peggy Landsman

NASTURTIUMS

Bright orange nasturtiums capture my awareness.
I lose myself in the wilderness
Of their green shield-shaped leaves.

Whenever I see nasturtiums, I see you.
Dark green glasses occult your eyes,
Your lips are lavished in red.

"It keeps my confidence up," you explain.
"A woman should never look faded."

Your short wavy hair never sports gray,
But some variation on a theme by henna.
When I ask, all you say is,
"It comes from a most expensive bottle."

You come from Fiji. You wear a tiki.

"In my day, men were men,
And women were double-breasted!
The boys all called me Coconut Ella."

Whenever I see nasturtiums, I hear you:
"Toss some in your salad," you tell me.
"They add a bit of color and they taste like onions."

The morning of your funeral, I kneel in your garden;
Use my kitchen scissors, cut myself a handful.

And all that impossible afternoon
Aboard that Neptune Society ship,
As we plow through the Bay to where it meets the Pacific,
I cling to those green stems until it is time to scatter them.
Your nasturtiums drift away.
Your ashes turn the water smoky for an instant.

But bugger all (as you would say)! I almost forgot:
The Blue Angels flew that day.
You would have liked them a lot.
Like you, they flaunted all they had,
A free display, not half bad,
The best send-off you could have had.

And Bob's your uncle...I won't whinge.
We sang all your bawdy songs, did our share of boozing.

"When I drink champagne," you loved to say,
"I feel I'm lying naked on golden sands,
Sea foam spilling like millions of pearls over my body. . .
But when I drink beer, I burp."

Your feather boa, ukulele strum...
Wherever you were, Ella, the party had begun.

Those Benson & Hedges cigarettes you used to smoke—
Your lipstick lingered on each filter like a kiss.

You kept my worst secrets. . .
Told me where you hid your extra keys and money.

Bright orange nasturtiums won't settle down.
They flutter their green leaves like fans.
Their delicate petals trumpet details,
All as solid as memory until my memory fails. . .

nasturtiums
falling
from
my hand

John Laue

THE FUNERAL SERVICE

Noel next door was afraid to leave the house
without her husband Rick.
He told her what to do; she obeyed.

Then 80 year old Rick's diabetes worsened;
his right leg was amputated
two inches above the knee.

From his wheelchair he declared,
I'm not going to live like this;
it's time for me to check out,
but I don't want any damn sky-pilot
bullshitting over me. Will you do my funeral?

Reluctant to refuse a friend,
especially one so close to death,
I agreed. Then Rick passed away.

As he wished, I prepared a service
with no prayers or God references,
and thought I'd lend a special touch
by including a famous haiku.

In front of neighbors gathered
next door at the funeral, I offered the poem:
The old pond. A frog jumps in. Plop!

Noel and most of the group

looked at me as if
I'd dropped a bomb in their midst.

Afterward my wife asked,
Why did you agree to do Rick's funeral?
And why did you use that poem?

I'm a poet, not a funeral director, I replied.
They should have expected more
than just an ordinary service.

A few days later Noel got a minister
to conduct a second service
complete with prayers and Bible readings,
something Rick would have hated,
but what she'd yearned for all the time.

Tina Lincer

IN THE MIDDLE

After my 94-year-old mother died, she was buried beside my father in a big Jewish cemetery on Long Island, a short distance from my Queens, N.Y., hometown. My family had purchased plots in the 1970s with other members of their cousins' club.

A few weeks after my mother's death, her sister died. At 86, Aunt Rita had been enjoying canasta and early bird specials on the east coast of Florida, so her sudden passing was a shock. Though I hadn't seen her in years, I'd always felt an emotional bond with my aunt. We were both outgoing, adventuresome women who'd moved away from home and our older sisters with little fanfare or regret.

Now Rita was coming back to New York to be buried. But where? My cousin told me my aunt was supposed to be laid to rest next to my parents, yet neither she nor her siblings could find the required cemetery paperwork.

There were four plots in my late father's name. He and my mother occupied two. Were the remaining two unnamed plots intended for my sister and me — or for my aunt and uncle?

My sister had cared for my parents until their deaths, and I assumed she would be buried with them. Not me. I'd be upstate, where I live with my longtime partner. I have always been the odd one out in my family.

In Judaism, we bury quickly; usually within three days after death. The clock was ticking. With my aunt's body in transit north, my cousins were entreating me to authorize the cemetery to use one of our plots, which now legally belonged to me and my sister. My sister, an eccentric who didn't use a computer or phone, wasn't equipped to take care of this.

For two days, I thought of nothing but my aunt's burial. It quickly became clear that if I gave away one plot for my aunt, I'd have to relinquish the other for my uncle someday. This would make my sister the odd one out.

My parents' cemetery, less than 10 miles from Kennedy Airport, is an old, crowded city of the departed. Narrow, one-way avenues give way to rows, sections, blocks and grave numbers. I began to wonder: Could I purchase one more plot?

"Don't worry. We'll bring your sister upstate," my partner joked. "Fresher air, easier for us to visit." He was trying to lighten my mood, but I remained tense. I was out of time.

I'd never know for sure what my parents' intention was for those two open plots, and I anguished over possibly giving away my sister's spot. Unlike me, she never married or had kids. I'd had no control over where she ended up in life, but now I was responsible for deciding where she'd be in death. Depriving her of a place beside our parents felt awful.

Yet my cousins needed me, and in the end, I decided to help them. My aunt and my mother had died without being on speaking terms. At least they'd be together in death.

My partner, sister and I attended my aunt's funeral service but skipped the burial. I was relieved my sister wouldn't see my aunt's casket lowered next to my parents.

Four weeks after my aunt died, I got word my uncle had passed away. I couldn't face another funeral. I was still stressed over managing my mother's tangled estate and helping my sister to live on her own for the first time at 65. All I wanted was to curl up and ignore the world.

"No pressure," my cousin said. Then she told me she'd finally found her parents' cemetery paperwork.

"It turns out my parents were in the same section but not in the plots that are in your father's name. So we are going to bury my father in his rightful place, and they'll move my mother later."

First I signed the interment papers, and now I signed the disinterment forms. Weeks later, I got a text from my cousin: "Wanted you to know everything was taken care of." On a warmer-than-usual East Coast winter day, Aunt Rita had been dug up and moved beside her husband.

It was a great unburdening. I immediately shed my guilt over taking the plot out from under my sister. And while I felt a twinge of sadness over my mother and aunt being separated again, at least both my aunt and I were out of the middle of this family drama.

◆ ◆ ◆

Claire Loader

FAMILY FLOWERS ONLY

A hush descends on the room, the silence waiting eagerly for the solemn, the monotone to start its daily chorus. A pause, a breath, and this curiosity from the heart of rural Ireland begins its mournful dance; muted, purposeful tones floating gracefully to sate the ears of its audience, as ghosts from the past make their last goodbyes.

Time feels suspended as the list gets read, one by one, the names filtering through the airwaves into memory, sparking the fires of days gone by, the hall dances, the socials, a chance encounter at the mart. *"He was a good man, he was a kind man..."* As are all men in death, washed with the same brush, so as not to stir the hereafter.

"Mary Margaret Connelly, reposing at Regan's funeral home, Galway..."

A sudden gasp of recognition, so many names the same, but a née and a location stills the heart. Not the Mary we knew now. Another, whose family will be busy today, buying in the tea, making the sandwiches. For mortality cannot be contemplated without them. Sorrow must be drowned - tea the long-held method of choice. Save the whiskey for the evening, when the crowds disperse, when tales of truth are told.

The announcer reads out the final notice, the words spoken slowly, as if allowing them to sink into the very fabric of the seats pulled close in to hear them:

Family flowers only, by request..."

A gap, a sigh, a moment of silence before the organ beats: that is all for today.

Heads lean back on chairs, feet fall quietly away from the radio, as time begins again and the broadcaster's voice, grave and somber, offers her condolences before the music starts once more.

♦♦♦

Fran Markover

FINAL ENTERPRISE

She doesn't want satin-covered pillows
or eulogies from a strange man of the cloth.
Nixes ashes in urns. She's past hot flashes.
Is too allergic for eco-villages of the dead,
no-frill cotton shrouds unsuitable for cold.
Instead, she favors a Starfleet traditional.
Her body placed in a torpedo casing launched
into outer space, some beefy Captain Kirk
conducting the ceremony, someone familiar
with enigmas and mythologies of the cosmos.
With bagpipes wheezing melancholy, prayer
flags could whip in wind, much like grandma's
fresh-washed socks fanning the sunflowers.
A chorus of angels offering melodic farewells,
like school friends who sing Amazing Grace
in their choir robes for hometown services
while she's beamed, no gravity, toward stars.

Kerry Dean Martinez

A STAINED-GLASS POEM

Joe knew he would soon be checking out. And it shocked him. He had death placed way in the future and here it was in the immediate. Always liking things to be a certain way, he had specifics about how he wanted his funeral. He talked about it and let me know where he wanted it to be, to swear not to put him in a suit, and to make it a rather grand affair. Open casket, cremation, get a niche, and move the ashes of his Mom and Dad and sister who died before him, in with him.

When he died, I went down to the chapel of the Chimes and started to plan the best funeral I could. It was strange because I had never appreciated or liked funerals before, but I was feverishly engaged in this one. I had a vision. I think it may have kept me sane. It seemed to take me over and I was glad for that.

As I met with the funeral team, I began to insist on no suit for Joe. The guy in charge of this assured me with a smile, that Joe had come to see him a few weeks ago and left specific instructions and made him promise. I asked what the instructions were, and they were the same ones Joe had given me. Work shirt, denim work pants, black work shoes. This was Joe's basic uniform. He did not want to be dressed up, he wanted people's last sight of him to be in his usual get up. I wore a denim shirt to his funeral in solidarity. He had told me not to wear black.

I dreaded the idea of an open casket, but I cherished the idea of putting his last wishes into action.

Music was important to Joe and to me. I had the help of my friend Sheba who found a wonderful singer. She sang her heart out for us all. *When I Lay My Burden Down.* Perfect for a hard-working man who died on Labor Day. She also did *Precious Lord, Take my Hand.* Joe loved *Amazing Grace*, so we had a pianist play a country church version as the guests came in. My friend Dan is a pastor and I met with him to let him know some of Joe's traits that were not so well known. How he would help the most difficult and broken. Those whose bridges had been burned. Those that most of us did not want to know. Instead of the regular funeral-bible stuff, I wanted Joe's holy side to be the focus.

The Chapel itself is an Oakland treasure. It was designed by Julia Morgan (who also designed San Simeon) and it was completed in the late-1920s. It is a major landmark and a beautiful structure. Lots of wood and glass.

One sister did the eulogy. I was grateful for that. Another sister did the program. Grateful for that too. Joe's brother-in-law wanted to read from the scriptures and I said, Okay, but a short hopeful one and not a preachy one. He did.

Joe's brother had dropped off the work clothes.

A bugler from the Navy came and played. Fitting since Joe was a Vietnam Era Veteran. I was presented with a flag and I gave it to the brother that Joe *Taps* argued with the most.

Joe loved flowers. He had amazing roses in his yard. Big pink ones, smaller watercolor looking ones and flaming orange ones. He loved tropical flowers. At his funeral, I had many huge displays of large, bright, tropical blooms behind his casket. A riot of color. Oranges, yellows, reds, purples.

Mariachi Colima (we knew them—they had played both for Joe's mother's birthday party and at our wedding party) came in the chapel in full fancy white regalia and played the classic Mexican goodbye funeral songs including *Las Golondrinas*.

After, we had a big banquet in a local restaurant and a huge *tres leches* cake for dessert. I remember going to our favorite bakery with Ramona and picking it up in her car and bringing it to the restaurant before the funeral. Sheba's husband put together a playlist from song titles I had given him and played them on his equipment throughout the dinner. Sam Cooke, Fats Domino, Los Lobos . . ..

At the end, I was happy that It all turned out right. That I had done my very best to make it Joe's own and not a pre-designed affair.

I also learned to look at funerals differently.

I loved having specific instructions. I loved making it his—just right for an earthy guy who was truly Mexican and truly American. The singer was 13. It was her first paid gig.

When I bring this day to mind—and I do, almost daily—it is a ritual mind movie. A poem with stained glass. An ode of love and pride. A tribute.

A big *adios* to my Mr. Joe!

◆◆◆

José Miramontes

EL DÍA DE LOS MUERTOS

It's certainly correct to say that José Luis, my firstborn child, is always very close to me on *El Día de los Muertos*, Mexico's Day of the Dead, which falls on November 2 each year. It's also true of the day before that when we specifically remember the children who have died. And it's true that he is with me every day.

Like many in my town near Guadalajara, I spend day and night during the ancient observance of *El Día de los Muertos* at the cemetery, where—in a very real sense—I visit with my boy. Like many, I prepare the grave in symbolic ways to honor him, and to receive the thousands of people who will visit the cemetery to connect with their own loved ones and ancestors. Throughout the observance, the cemetery will be transformed with lavishly decorated gravesites and makeshift altars covered with marigolds and other flowers, and perhaps families will gather at graveside over a favorite meal or traditional foods and drinks they share with the departed.

It has been this way for centuries, since long before the Spaniards arrived, bringing a new religion that added its own elements while still preserving the ancient indigenous ones. At its heart, *Día de los Muertos* is a living expression of our understanding that those we have loved and lost, and those who came before us, continue to live among us and touch our lives.

For me, *El Día de los Muertos* is one way to remind José Luis that we are present, just as he is present in my life not only that day but every day. As a small child, as a young boy coping with a terrible disease, and in the years since we lost him, he has been my teacher.

José Luis was only twelve years old when he died, twelve years ago in a Guadalajara hospital, and five years after his leukemia was first diagnosed and our painful journey began.

Until the night he became very ill he had always been a happy and healthy boy. He was a good student with a lot of friends, and he liked to play soccer and climb and hike in the mountains alongside our town. In every way, he was a wonderful, good boy.

His illness came on suddenly, and we were immediately thrown into a frustrating and ultimately heartbreaking quest to get him the treatment that might have saved him. It took six different doctors to get a diagnosis, and years of fighting and pleading with the medical bureaucracy in hopes of getting him the bone marrow transplant that was his best hope for survival.

Both of his younger brothers were compatible as bone marrow donors and, thanks to a generous community, the large amount of money needed to pay for the procedure was available. But everything from hospital protocols to lengthy waiting lists blocked the way. I knocked on doors and they closed the doors on me. By the time a friend from the U.S. helped connect us to a Texas hospital that would perform the transplant, his disease had progressed too far for it to be successful.

At the end, José Luis spent a month in the hospital. He was there on April 30, the day that Mexico celebrates *El Día Del Niño*, Children's Day. To mark the day for the children confined to hospital beds, staff members handed out small gifts, a set of toy cars for José Luis. I encouraged him to play with them, but he told me, "Where I'm going, I'm not going to need them." He died that day.

I was devastated, and for weeks afterward I didn't want to live. But, as I said before, José Luis teaches me. He came to me one night in a dream and asked, "Hey, Dad. When are you going to come?" My dream self answered, "On time."

I can't say where that answer came from, but it helped me understand that we would be together again someday. I don't know when that will be, but I know now that it will be "on time." And until that time, I know that he will always remain present.

These are some of the thoughts and memories I carry into the cemetery on *El Día de los Muertos* to spend time with my son at his lovingly decorated grave, complete with a small topiary hedge that spells out his name. It's an important and beautiful tradition in my culture, and one that reminds us that those who have died still have much to teach us, the living.

◆ ◆ ◆

Sheryl L. Nelms

THE FUNERAL AT MINGUS, TEXAS

they said
Bobbie Lou

paid for them to do it
her way at the cemetery

blue tarp
roof

live band

and her
right there

in her pink coffin
on the stand

over the grave

while they
line danced
did the Cotton-Eyed Joe

and swigged

cases
of Pearl
and Lone Star

that she bought before she died

then tossed
their empties

into the hole
before they
lowered

her away

Bonnie Neubauer

DUST IN THE WIND

I was initially fine with my husband's 'no funeral' request. I spooned a portion of his ashes into a pouch for his sister, sealed a tiny amount into a locket for myself, stashed the funeral home bag in his closet, and shut the door.

As the weeks crawled by, I couldn't silence the part of my heart that wanted to honor Gil. Whenever I drove by places that had been meaningful in our relationship – the bakery where we got our wedding cake, the bookstore where we met, the dealership where we shopped for an RV– I thought how nice it would be if a part of Gil were there.

I hatched a plan, a ritual, that I named 'Dropping Ashes'. I approached it with the enthusiasm of a dog, marking our territory every chance I got, and the stealth of a graffiti artist, only 'dropping' at night.

One of my first 'drops' was outside a helicopter museum. Standing under an aircraft carrier in the dark, arm straight by my side, I subtly dropped ashes, and spoke aloud, "When you chose this spot after 9-11 as our safe place to meet-up, I felt protected. Since you died, I haven't felt safe anywhere. Knowing you are here, now, I feel a bit better. I miss you like crazy. I love you." I cried in my car for an hour.

A couple weeks later I was driving aimlessly in the Pocono Mountains of Pennsylvania, hoping a scenery change would soothe my grief. It had not, and the sun was starting to set. But I didn't want to go home. What was at home? A half-empty bed? Unfinished dreams?

When Gil was dying, a hospice social worker said, "Bonnie, for Gil, home is where you are." These were kind words when I momentarily contemplated reneging on my promise to let him die at home. Now they stung. Where was home for me?

One of our pet expressions popped into my head, "It's only a ride until we make our first U-turn; then it's an adventure." Not certain it would be an adventure without Gil in the car, I turned anyway. I immediately knew where to go and queued up Gil's favorite ice cream parlor on the GPS. Only an hour out of the way; excellent news for someone who didn't want to go home.

Without worry of getting caught because the shop was closed for the season, I dropped ashes directly under Gil's favorite sign – a big, brightly lit milk carton.

Back in the car, one of our favorite road trip songs played on the radio: *Two of Us*. The Beatles sang, *"Two of us riding nowhere..."*

I yelled at the radio, "One of us. There's no more two." The radio kept playing, *"On our way back home... We're on our way home."*

I shouted, "I don't want to go home. There's no home anymore."

The radio insisted, *"We're on our way home. We're going home."*

I banged the steering wheel until my palms hurt, but still not as much as my heart. Between the rain and my wet eyes, I could barely see anything on the winding road. I drove on, anger that had been boiling under the surface raging from my mouth.

"I hate you for dying. I hate that stupid twinkle in your eye that made me fall in love with you. I hate how you always made me laugh when I was sad. What am I supposed to do now? Tell me, big boy. I'm sad. I'm angry. I'm alone. If you're out there, make me laugh. Please!"

The song changed. Kansas. *Dust in the Wind*.

"Gil?" I said hesitantly, "That's a cheap shot. I'm not laughing." Truth be told I was amused.

"I'm giving you one more chance. One more song to make me laugh. Let's see if you're listening."

When Kansas stopped singing, I sat up straight, eager to hear what Radio-Gil would play. I was half-certain it would make me laugh and half-petrified I was actually talking to Gil through the radio.

The next song was *Alone Again, Naturally*. By none other than GILBERT O'Sullivan. A smile spread across my lips. I laughed. A genuine, audible laugh.

"You win, Gil. We're going home. The two of us."

That was the last time I 'dropped' ashes. I had gotten what I had been craving, what funerals typically deliver: the chance to smile, laugh, cry, reminisce, and feel connected.

◆ ◆ ◆

Opeyemi Parham

A ONE IN A MILLION DEATH

She went into the earth on the land where she had once lived, shrouded in a favorite piece of cloth, six hours after her death. Compost and items from her garden were buried with her.

We had walked a wacky waltz of a three month path from her one-in-a-million diagnosis (Cruzfeld Jacob Disease) to her death. Suzy had noticed she was unable to remember her dreams, first. Less than two months later, she came to understand she was dying of a hundred percent fatal and rapidly progressive neurologic wasting disease.

That was the end of February.

She died on March 26.

Because Suzy—an Italian American social worker transplanted from small town Pennsylvania to rural Franklin County in Massachusetts over 40 years ago—was a quirky, funny, dramatic and extremely loving individual, her dying and her death rituals were just like her.

One in a million.

Suzy's political theater troupe had been the ones to organize the farewell party. While Suzy was still able to respond (although she was already aphasic and having choreiform movements), they had dreamed up a Great Gathering, planned for the local town hall. Suzy—dressed in red—arrived by wheelchair. She was transferred to a red velvet throne that someone had found in a prop room somewhere. From that throne, she had one-on-one moments to share love and goodbyes with her friends, who waited patiently in line the way one does for Santa Claus in a department store. She said her goodbyes for close to three hours. Some people laughed with her. Others cried. Others were too freaked out by the morbid circumstances to do anything but stand on the other side of the room by the food.

But they had come.

And, there were close to three hundred of us.

That party ended with Suzy being transferred back into her wheelchair and leaving the building to banjo music, all of us singing "Marching off to Freedomland."

The serious dying continued. Seventy-two individuals, always in pairs, mobilized for shifts so that Suzy spent her last month surrounded by friends. Five of those friends were physically present with her as she breathed her last breath. In her own home.

Suzy could best be described as a recovered Catholic, who sourced from Buddhism and eclectic paganism. So, first there was the Pagan bonfire at her grave site. Being a practicing Pagan myself, it was emotionally painful for me to witness a community of Franklin County Yankees attempting to execute ceremonial traditions that they did not understand. Calling the directions? Lighting a bonfire? Where were the hot dogs and the s'mores? How could I be the only one crying, as a regimentally attired bagpiper stood at the top of the hill playing Amazing Grace?   I imagine that Franklin County Yankee community was still simply too shocked to have much of an emotional reaction other than numbness. We were all doing the best we could, conscious dying being such a novel idea in this death phobic culture.

Thirty-nine days after her death (following Buddhist tradition), Suzy's Big Memorial Celebration occurred. The sea of emotionally constipated and repressed people who had surrounded me at the Pagan bonfire two weeks earlier had thawed. Held on a gorgeous piece of land on a bright Saturday in May, Suzy had requested a genuine second line jazz parade. About thirty of the two hundred attending the memorial service processed up a hill and through an archway of birch bark to a hill overlooking the memorial site. The archway was decorated with Suzy's amazing wardrobe. Brightly colored hats hung above our heads, knee-high red boots and other outrageous footwear were nailed along the sides of the arch and brightly colored scarves fluttered in a light breeze.

Jazzing that second line in a dance back down the hill, we joined the larger community for a more traditional, sit-down memorial service. Representatives from various aspects of Suzy's life each shared from the heart. Stories, of Suzy: the hippie food co-op organizer, the recovered drug addict, the sensitive social worker, the wacky actor, the lover and the overly available, sometimes codependent friend.

Perhaps due to that codependent tendency, but more likely a function of her Italian-American background, Suzy's last directive was that money from her life insurance policy go to a catered meal for the two hundred who showed up at her memorial service. No inadequate Yankee potlucks for this lady!

And, I was bequeathed one of the most outrageous hats in her collection.

James Penha

WAY TO GO

Instead of starving and smoking
himself to a slow suicide to free
himself of the diapers and falls,
the tumors and the pneumonias,
I should have invited my brother
to Sumatra where I would have
carried him through the rice
and corn fields to find a giant
reticulated python to embrace
him and enfold him and sleep
with him until my brother turned
instead of ash into a brave lattice
of living colors.

Herbert W. Piekow

THE BURIAL

Doña Maria de la Luz Rojas Mercado de Ramirez died Tuesday; because she was not embalmed she was buried the following day. All ten of her surviving children and numerous grandchildren arrived for the viewing. Most of her progeny reside in various parts of the US only three of her children live in Guadalajara. The ninety-year-old matriarch of this prodigious clan was prepared for her death_spiritually, mentally and physically. Although the notice of her demise was expected the pain and sorrow of her passing was not lessened.

The funeral bus to transport some family and friends departed the mortuary at exactly noon. The procession of cars following the hearse was long and slow. The funeral cortege passed by the home of Doña Luz so that the neighbors who were unable to attend the graveside services could wave goodbye. We arrived at the cemetery an hour after leaving the mortuary. The Pantheon Guadalajara covers approximately ten square city blocks. A five-piece mariachi band played quiet, but familiar music while we gathered at the entry gates. Leading the procession of mourners, the mariachi began to process up the cobbled road as_several of Doña Luz`s grandchildren took turns carrying the polished mahogany coffin, while we mourners shuffled along the rocky road, dust rose like beige talc. The mariachi continued to play their music which now sounded like a dirge.

"Oh my god. I shall never see you again," wailed an eighty-six-year-old sister, herself being supported by two of her adult children. A thin layer of grit covered each of us as we continued to march zombie like up the cobbled roadway while the mariachi played.

At last the group of mourners arrived, we formed ourselves in a semi-circle and stared at the opened grave. The mariachi assembled at the head and played another mournful tune. Two open sided white tarps shaded the grave; we mourners were left to lean against tombstones, while a few women produced umbrellas to provide a minimum of relief from the scorching heat of the sun. Like an apparition an elderly woman with a black mantilla cascading from the crown of her head and covering her face began to lead the assembly in praying the rosary. The mariachi provided comforting background music.

Carmen, who had taken care of her mother, rushed to the now opened_coffin; Her words flowed with sincerity as she thanked her mother for being the guide of the family and especially for giving her the honor to hold their mother when she drew her final breath. Carmen's three adult children went to the side of their grieving mother, while the mariachi played. The children began to massage their mother's neck with rubbing alcohol and splashed bottled water on their fainting mother's face.

From across the grave a niece pushed her way to the coffin crying in a loud voice, "*Perdoname tia por haberte heho sentir mal.*" As the adult niece petitioned for forgiveness the mariachi fell silent and our attention was shifted to a grandson, the size of a gorilla, a tattoo of rattlesnake, fangs opened and ready to strike wound its way down the bulging bicep of his right arm as he stormed over to the gravediggers who were distracting the prayers. A few well-spoken words and respect was restored. The mariachi picked up where they left off and a swirl of ghost dust rose from the dry ground.

As Doña Luz´s coffin disappeared into the dry earth alongside her husband and a son the mariachi played the last mournful tune, *"Hay que Morir para vivir,"* "We need to die so that we may live."

◆ ◆ ◆

Herbert W. Piekow

THE CRYPT

A week after the burial a contractor was hired to build a small structure over the family graves. All permits were obtained and the Pantheon Guadalajara allowed one week for the construction. The contractor worked two days then suddenly abandoned the project. After a futile search for another contractor Gustavo, the youngest son and I volunteered to complete the task. I had helped my stepfather with numerous rock walls and other home projects. Gustavo prayed to his parents to contact his grandfather to let him borrow his hands to finish the project. Don Jose, the first to be buried in the family plot, was a well-known brick layer and Gustavo asked his grandfather to bless the hands that were to build a family monument. After purchasing the materials we needed, the original contractor had everything, we began. A rough brick understructure had been completed earlier and we needed to smooth over the rough spots, apply the Sea of Cortez blue colored tiles and finish the project to pass inspection by the cemetery board. For three days Gustavo and I mixed mortar, wiped our brows in the broiling sun, cut and applied tiles. On the third and final day we patiently wiped away excess mortar, washed down the entire edifice, and added a final touch of fresh flowers to surround the crypt .We stood up and admired the family resting place, prayed to those buried there and thanked Gustavo´s grandfather. The inspection committee approved the family mausoleum.

◆ ◆ ◆

Holly Pruett

OPERATOR, COULD YOU HELP ME PLACE THIS CALL?

"I to her every day," my friend says, of her her who died last year.

always been more tongue tied.

Not with the living, usually, but with the dead.

Imagined conversations, remembered conversations— my thoughts are filled with these, exchanges with my father, my Nonna, my friends Bill, Marcy, Kathy, and others

But to speak out loud--to them, to those who came before them, whose lives collectively, cumulatively, ended up as me—is to render me shy, uncertain, inept. is to render me shy, uncertain, inept.

I used a song to unscrew my jaw when I knew I needed to say certain things to my dad at the memorial I held for him in my backyard eight months after he died.

Operator, well could you help me place this call?
'Cause I can't read the number that you just gave me.
There's something in my eyes,
You know it happens every time
I think about the love I thought would save me.

Jim Croce (1943-1973) was the soundtrack to those fifth- and sixth-grade years when my father left us again and again for an affair he was unable to break off. And then he left for good, moving six thousand miles away six days after his divorce from my mother was final on my twelfth birthday.

I bought two copies of Croce's Greatest Hits twenty-five

years later when my dad was diagnosed with terminal brain cancer: one for him, one for me. Already unable to do many things for himself, he shrugged his consent when I offered to put it on the stereo. We wept through nearly every song. Those around us were badly discomfited. But I like to think that he and I, in those tear-soaked moments, were speaking the same language for perhaps the first time.

Croce's *Operator* sang through my mind again as I cast myself back to my dad's death earlier this month, on the fifteenth anniversary of that life-altering day.

A friend sent me a link to an episode of *This American Life* featuring a phone booth in northeastern Japan serving as a memorial to those dead (nearly 17,000) and missing (still more than 2,500) in the earthquake and tsunami. Dubbed Telephone of the Wind, it's connected (by phone company standards) to nowhere. And yet individuals of all ages and whole family groups are making pilgrimages from all over the country to stand in the structure overlooking the sea, pick up the black rotary-dial telephone receiver, and speak aloud.

Hello. If you're out there please listen to me.

According to one article, "The phone is owned by a 70-year-old gardener named Itaru Sasaki who had installed the phone in his garden prior to the disaster in order to give him a private space to help him cope with the loss of his cousin."

After the tsunami struck a wider public became aware of the phone, and the site was attracting some thousands of visitors a year before long.

Listening to the Japanese-American radio journalist translate documentary recordings of these conversations, I was struck by how hard it can be to loosen one's tongue when the listener is on the other side of the veil. Even in Japan, where the "idea of keeping up a relationship with the dead is not such a strange one," as explained by reporter Miki Meek, citing the ancestor altar her uncle maintains: "There are photos on a little platform and every day he leaves fresh fruit and rice for them, lights incense, and rings a bell. It's a way to stay in touch. To let them know they are still a big part of our family."

Even there, it might take a simple rotary phone to loosen the tongue, to speak words carried by breath to those who are no longer breathing, but who nevertheless are not gone.

Isn't that the way they say it goes
But let's forget all that
And give me the number if you can find it
So I can call just to tell them I'm fine and to show
I've overcome the blow.
I've learned to take it well
I only wish my words could convince myself
That it just wasn't real
But that's not the way it feels
No . . .no . . . no . . . no.

♦ ♦ ♦

For the complete lyrics to *Operator (that's not the way it feels)* as well as complete information about the late singer-songwriter's legacy, see www.jimcroce.com.

Tony Reevy

BUCKLE UP

The weight beside me
trips on the *passenger seat*
occupied indicator.

My car beeps,
the *seat belt*
unfastened light
blinks red.

In the faux marble
container, nothing
but "homogenized" dust.

Still, like the director
suggested, I wrap
the seatbelt around Mom—
her last ride—
and strap her in.

Carlos Reyes

I SELDOM GO TO FUNERALS

Just the sound
of the one pebble

from the first shovel—
ful of dirt

hitting the
lacquered top

The echo
swallowed

by the earth—
tells me why

Natalie Safir

UNVEILING THE STONE

A light cheesecloth concealed the stone next to her husband's—an austere decorated monument placed nine years earlier in a vast populated field—obedient soldiers standing at attention displaying the required identities and inscriptions. One stone along the path bore only a name partly rubbed away by wind and tears—eleven hollow letters left to signify a life.

When the scanty veil was lifted to reveal a rosy marble headstone, it seemed to me too soon, barely months since my dear friend's burial. A woman rabbi intoned the Kaddish prayer to the group of onlookers—three sons and their wives, one couple and many children. The sons stood closest—a practicing Jew, a Catholic with uncertain beliefs, and a Buddhist who had married a South Asian lawyer.

My friend, raised in Ireland as a Catholic, many years back had gone through all the required rituals, traditional rites to become an American Jew. Had her three sons bar mitzvahed to conform with her husband's faith and hers newly found. *Amazing, the way it turned out*, she said, remarking to me one day on her thirteen grandchildren. *It's a hodgepodge of colors and beliefs*. I felt her heavy sigh of both awe and ambivalence. *Mostly boys*, she said, *and yet, I worry that our name will not be carried forward*.

One by one, the line of thirteen children repeating their parents' gestures, placed tokens selected by their small hands on top of their grandmother's stone. *To show that you came here to honor her*, a mother explained to the bewildered child struggling to understand permanence and mortality now that

Nana was permanently gone. *We learned it from our Hebrew ancestors,* she continued, trying to invoke this ancient code to her son, raised Catholic. The sapling boy, Nathan was the most difficult to console, his streaked face showing a veil of pain. *You were her favorite,* I whispered inching toward him, hoping in vain to alleviate his suffering.

The crafted monument's geometry and heft suggested permanence. The quality of solid marble conformed to generations of tradition. Yet standing there in the cold as snow fell covering the field, I remember my poet friend's mercurial nature, her need to fly and shift with the seasons, her desire to be one with the elements. I wish they knew her as I did—surely a fragrant slender perennial would have suited her better.

After the oldest son read one of her poems he carried on his cellphone, I quoted a few of her lines: *we're rumors flying down star lanes, memories lost in the smoke of galaxies* and felt her spirit grazing my shoulders. Her family looked at me and puzzled the lines. Perhaps they also pondered the woman who had written them.

Kenneth Salzmann

THE PERSISTENCE OF ASHES

In fact, it is the roses that remain.

They enter the house all summer long,
and longer. I place them on the mantle beside the urn
where they will expend their pinks and reds petitioning
what gods they know for the persistence of your ashes.

And they will weep petals across the hearth.

At times, I catch myself believing in the immutability
of ashes, as if we are of this place or any other. As if
the generations that go on spreading like ash will turn
one day to the fixed notion of a place that is home.

The roses were planted fifty years ago or more,
a neighbor said, by a woman who went about, as people do,
growing flowers and growing old, until there was nothing
left but roses to testify that she had ever been.
And we set out to make a home amid the thorns
and petals of her life. We nested in the oak-lined rooms
that remembered all her moods and all her movements,
but only briefly. And you took it upon yourself to nurture
those roses, perhaps in hopes of sanctifying a transitory
life followed seamlessly by ash and bone.

Kenneth Salzmann

SMALL ROUND WORDS

I am about to stop writing
about my dead.
The poems are piling up
in plain pine boxes,
they're lining unmarked graves
and fluttering like ash
above the redbricked chimney
of the Woodlawn crematorium;
always, I am leaving
small round words like stones
upon the crypt.

Gerard Sarnat

Castro Hours Back Then

Riffing off Cleve Jones,
muse of the AIDS quilt,
the world's largest
ever community
art project, after
listening to his
fabulous fairy
tale interview
on *Fresh Air*
this mourning:

Gypsy taxicabs,
highway of death,
perhaps worst place
my blood-spattered
eyes have so far seen,
those colorful mothers of
mostly lovely men with
Kaposi's sarcoma huff
into town. After our flat's
furniture gets sold,
I am tossed onto
that street -- now
to contemplate
three by six
feet panels
gravesize.

Mary Ann Savage

WHAT REMAINS

My husband's ashes are on top of his bureau in a pretty ceramic urn. It weighs about nine pounds. They say that when you are cremated, you go back to your birth weight. Every time Bud's brother or cousins call, they ask, very kindly, what I plan to do with him. Bill would like some of his ashes in a small container. I want to answer, "Have them all." But that would be crass and would seem as if I didn't care.

Well, I don't. Neither my mate nor his spirit resides in that dignified red container. And no, having him there in the room we shared doesn't "creep me out" as some people have asked. If I want to invoke his presence, that comes to me when I see his old blue bathrobe which still hangs in hid side of the closet, or when one of his favorite reruns is on the tv screen. Or in any one of his habits, the little chores I now do alone, like making sure the curtains are open. And when I make the same pot of coffee I always brewed for us, which is exactly twice what I drink. Or when the house settles and I think I've heard him in another room.

It has been a year now, and so much of him is still imprinted on the house. I "ought" to move the furniture, get out more, donate his Lazy Boy chair . . . make a new life. Sometimes friends express the idea that I'm in some kind of denial, wanting things to stay the same. I deny that. This has been my home too, through the years. To arbitrarily change things so I won't be reminded seems disrespectful, somehow.

Between the waves of grief, indifference, and general loss, I like living alone, the freedom of only having to watch my own diet, activities. There's a freedom, an autonomy in that, and not making changes means I can still find my way around the house in the dark.

We had a sweet, sentimental, very traditional memorial, with tributes of all kinds. Our daughter sang *Amazing Grace*. and we had what Bud always wanted, a jazzy rendition of *When the Saints Come Marching In* at the end. It was traditional, but still very individual to his taste. We had a reception at a favorite upscale Mexican Restaurant, with lots of food, shared memories, toasts.

After a year, I suppose it's time for another ritual. It would be easy to scatter Bud's ashes in the ocean, saving a little for anyone who wanted that. It would be better, though, to do it at the lake he loved, where he grew up, and most of the memories are. I hope I can arrange that in the coming months. But I don't think it's a ritual I need, personally. I have all the remembrances I need. I carry his heart in my heart.

◆◆◆

Patti See

MOURNING PORTRAIT

The night before Mom's funeral, I sit at my kitchen counter drinking beer and listening to audio recordings I made before she stopped speaking a year ago. Each time I recorded Mom and Dad I'd come home and listen, usually like this, late at night.

Mom died on Thursday, and now it's Sunday. These past four weeks, I haven't gone a day without seeing her. Tomorrow I'll touch my mother for the last time. I can't wrap my mind around that, so I sit at the counter and let her voice fill my kitchen. This is my wake.

Years ago Dad decided to offer a two-hour "visitation" before Mom's funeral, so everything was in one day. "Not enough tears for *two* days," he chuckled, using his humor to acknowledge how exhausting it is to mourn and greet the public at his age.

Traditionally a wake the night before a funeral was to view the body of a loved one and keep watch over it, usually at home. In some cultures, a wake allowed time to make sure the person was truly dead. Sometimes a bell was attached to the body with string so family would hear if the person stirred.

Mom once told me the most afraid she'd ever been as a child was when her parents were laid out in their coffins in the family living room. 1938. 1942. I never knew to ask if Mom lay in bed with her sisters, all night listening for a tinkling of the bell that meant these untimely deaths—cancer, car accident—had been a horrific mistake.

As a child I found "coffin photos" of these grandparents in our attic, keepsakes Mom could not part with, though she would never display them. She owned just one other photo of her parents, a wedding portrait. I remember my sidelong glances at these dead bodies. Though I didn't know the word then, only one fits: macabre.

When I leave my house the morning of Mom's funeral, I pass Slim's Saddle Bar, where the barstools used to be topped with real saddles until some drunk fell off and sued. Even before 9 am there's a group on the front porch smoking cigarettes. They are just off the 11 to 7 shift, I'd guess, and drinking before bed. No one knows I'm on the way to my mother's funeral; it's just another Monday to the rest of the world.

In the church vestibule I gather with Dad and my seven siblings, their spouses, children and grandchildren.

"I've got Mom's purse with me today," I say to my sister. I hold it up.

"I'm wearing her dress," another sister says. A lovely navy blue print from 1950 or so, when Mom was a size five.

"I'm wearing her earrings," another says. These are sweet tributes, part of our own ceremony, though none of us told the others we planned this.

"I'm *not* wearing her underwear," a sister says. We all laugh.

My son and his cousins go out to the hearse to get their grandma. Last night we estimated the weight: if Mom is 80 pounds and the casket is 220, then six grandkids can sure lift fifty pounds each.

When they carry her in, a sister says, "Well there she is," as if Mom's been missing.

The pallbearers rest the casket on a cart and push Mom up to the altar. The Horan brothers open her casket for our family viewing. This is the moment I have dreaded: seeing her "laid out." Her casket seems too small to hold a body. My hands feel enormous. Everything is slightly fuzzy around the edges. For a moment I think I might pass out.

I stand next to Dad. I hear a brother suck in his breath and walk away. We've got about thirty minutes with Mom until guests start to arrive. *Let's just get through this*, is all I can think.

"She's pretty," I say to no one in particular.

Dad didn't want anyone to photograph Mom her last two weeks of life, given her lack of dentures and empty stare. Today, she is beautiful. Anyone who knows her knows this isn't how she looked, but she *is* lovely. The Horan brothers have filled in her cheeks—no longer the hollowed out features of someone who forgot how to swallow—and they've given her back her large bust.

"Who brought a camera?" Dad says.

"I did," I tell him.

He says, "Now you can take her picture."

◆◆◆

Linda Simone

TRIPTYCH

S ince I'll be dead anyway, I'm not overly concerned about plans for my wake and funeral. Whoever is left can do what they please: a photo montage; playing Dave Brubeck's "Take Five" as mourners file into the funeral parlor; perhaps a reading of one of my signature poems, probably "If You've Never Stepped in Dog Poop" (I'm not kidding) in a church I've never attended. I sincerely hope people will be joyful and not morose because as I draw closer to my 70th birthday, my life so far has been pretty darn good.

Once the expected rituals are over, my choice is to be cremated, with my ashes divided and released in three ways. I ask that the first third of my remains be tossed over the Hartsdale Pet Cemetery in Westchester, New York, to mingle with the ashes of Charley, my ever-loyal and beloved mixed terrier of 16-1/2 years. As death wishes go, this is probably not too far-fetched. When it came time to send my pet to the great doggie-beyond, the vet promised Charley's ashes would be spread in the cemetery. Let's hope the vet was diligent. (Sorry if this sounds like a Stephen King novel.)

The second third of what's left of me, I'd like spread across Shakespeare's Garden in New York City's Central Park not far from the Delacorte Theater. I've delighted in many performances of Shakespeare in the Park, so maybe I can still catch a few lines of iambic pentameter. Hopefully, my ashes will fertilize the colorful wildflowers in the Bard's garden, and who knows where bits of me will land, carried on the wings of butterflies! With any luck, some spectacular stained-glass Monarch will make sure that a smattering of my ashes combine with some of my husband's ashes (when his time comes), which also will be floating around Central Park.

That leaves the final third, which I request to be sprinkled in San Antonio's Japanese Tea Garden. The Tea Garden is special to me, beautiful, peaceful, and just what I needed to help me transition four years ago to San Antonio as my second home. The pagoda, lily pond, koi, waterfalls—and the story of the immigrant family who once lived there—all inspired poems that eventually led to *The River Will Save Us*, my first full-length poetry collection. If you're a poet, you'll understand that once you snag a publisher for your work, you can finally die happy.

I realize that these last wishes will entail booking a trip to New York for my family. I hope after they dispose of my ashes, they'll take in the latest Broadway blockbuster play. I hope they'll enjoy a fine ethnic dinner and raise a glass to me and every other creature, animal or human, whom they loved and who, with me, will be blowing in the wind.

◆◆◆

Richelle Lee Slota

MY I'M-GOING-TO-DIE-TODAY-TO-DO LIST

1. Empty my pockets.

2. Stiff stupid stuff: the gym, vitamins, vacuuming.

3. Dig. The world is full of people indifferent to the ditches
   I have dug. Time to dig another ditch and lay down in it.

4. Say goodbye. I have said numberless false goodbyes
   to those I love. This goodbye is true.

Joseph Stanton

LANIKAI SEA BURIAL

It could be a dream: this cool, gray dawn,
this cathedral of sea and beach, holding
us hushed and sad under vast flying
buttresses of limestone-colored cloud,
the sun rising to rose window as we wait,
the waves cresting their sullen mahogany.
At first conch-trumpeting
five densely woven garlands of maile lei
unfurl along a line of family hands,
making a slice of beach a green aisle to the sea.
The rising tide slaps the bared feet
of his daughters' hula halau,
surging a counterpoint to their sway of song:
something about the sea and a feeling for it.

His sons lift and parade the ceramic shape
his form has come down to.
Precision stoke on stroke carries them out
to where the glitter of breaking light
can dance with flakes of his shadow,
trailing in the gentle tug of the careful canoe,
which circles and recircles the tiny, flat island
the old man had always loved to swim for.
No one can remember
if this low nub of landfall has a name.
Some flakes swirl back towards shore;
others float out, headed for Japan or further.
It will take years to get there.

Alison Stone

HUNGER

They have to wait to bury my mother
until my daughter stops nursing.
She had slept in a padded basket

while I stood wooden between my husband and my father;
people droned my mother's praises
and the coffin loomed.

Now she wakes and roots, all
hunger. A stranger takes us
to the rabbi's study. Amid clutter

of paper and books, I lift my black shirt. Broken,
numb, I cannot imagine my body
will respond, but her latch draws milk down.

She sucks dreamily. New to this world,
she knows nothing but a mother
who drips tears on her still-closing skull.

Her eyes flicker open and shut. Someone knocks,
asks me to hurry. I rub my daughter's back.
Her eyes stay closed now

but the fierce gums clamp.
I wait. The knot in my throat starts to soften.

As long as she holds on, nothing is final. The drive to the grave
postponed, my mother is still above ground, here
with her new grandchild and me.

Katherine Barrett Swett

CITY OF REFUGE

I dream we're exiled to a distant land,
a home for careless parents searching for
the lost, a place where locals understand
we'll never find what we had years before;
and when a stranger there makes idle chat,
we know he'll know that we have a dead child
or two and he does too and he'll know that
you talk about the dead as if alive.
For in the waking world we hesitate
to mention her; we have to make a choice
between our neighbor's staring at his plate
and somehow seeming to have lost his voice,
or our just saying that we have no daughter,
the way a drunk might say his gin was water.

Margaret Van Every

ECCE HOMO

The patriarch sleeps in his box at last,
or so we are asked to believe. We gather
to solemnize, to pay our last, to have a
terminal experience. We mime the gestures
of bereavement, but a grandchild asks why
no one is crying.
                              The lid must stay
shut, says she who made the arrangements;
he has not been cosmetically prepared.
But the same child who always
advertised the emperor's nakedness
demands to see for himself and,
to our wonder, the director allows
the opening.
                              No big deal, at
least to the director, but the suspense
for us is gothic. Some of us have
never seen a corpse and
we half expect him to rave at our
intrusion. An aura of the freak show
now sweeps the parlor, binding
the curious in conspiracy, though
each of us has our reasons. I recall
years ago having paid a quarter
to peer into such a box at the
state fair to see how the maiden
escaped the magician's daggers.
Now daggerless there he lies, a tad

smaller than we remember, no doubt
diminished by the recent ordeal, but all
in all, looking fine, though a bit wan.
In his white satin robe and cap, he's
innocent as a neonate cradled,
wanting nothing. Beyond beneficence
or harm, he's let us go.

Sandy Warren

SEND-OFF WITH A SONG

I absolutely, positively refuse to have a funeral. I don't go to other people's funerals, why the hell would I go to my own?

This is not a decision made in haste. My calculator says I've had 28,470 days and nights to ponder the subject.

In all that time, I've not come up with one good thing about funerals, and the bad things keep increasing. For example, last month I heard a TV pitchman for an insurance company warn viewers that the average cost of a funeral is $8,508. Would anyone really want to spend that much money, or any amount, on a ritual that brings folks to tears and certainly does no favors for the poor soul stretched out in the casket and gawked at by the curious?

In lieu of a funeral or anything remotely resembling one, I have prearranged my mini five-minute no frills remembrance celebration. It hinges on my friend Mac Rebennack, aka Dr. John, who was conceived nine months after me, outliving me. I think the chances are good. The famed singer and songwriter has been clean for 29 years, doesn't drink, eats what his nutritionist prescribes, and takes his meds. His only unhealthy habit is smoking a cigarette now and then. And, oh yes, he's from strong stock. His mother, Dorothy, lived to be in her nineties.

A few other things will need to be done before the celebration begins. I'm assuming I'll die calmly at home. I hate hospitals as much as I hate funerals. My senior citizen apartment building, where death is a common occurrence, has an untitled form on file for every tenant. I guess they don't want to call it the "death form." It states who the office will call when the resident dies. My form lists my son Tim.

As per my wish file stored in his safe, Tim will make some calls. After checking with Mikal's Funeral Parlor, he'll tell the Humanity Gifts Registry that my donated body will be deposited at the doorstep of whatever Philadelphia area medical school they specify, ASAP.

Next, he'll call Marie, Jane, and Jane Marie. They will notify the rest of my tribe.

Later, he'll send everybody one of my haiku on a little card the size of a business card:

I have danced at Jazz Fest
And dined on lobster from the sea.
Think I'll rest a while.

Sandy, 1940—the present

Tim's final call will be to Mac. My soulful friend, my muse, will go to the closest piano and play a tune for me. This gesture, which will take only minutes, will nurture me eternally. The Earth will feel the beat and turn on its axis.

♦ ♦ ♦

Sarah Brown Weitzman

THE HIVE

It throbs in an outer wall of a museum.
On display, the nest, bees and dank honey

are one vibrating hub. Bee-over-bee balls
of bees wrinkle and smooth as their black shine

worms in cells and out. But I won't press
against the glass to hear the whir of drones within.

I know that din. The day my father had a stroke
and could not speak, his bee box came

square, white and locked. While he died
I sat beside that box. I understood the hum

of fury sealed in. I heard the wearing away
of wings against those coffin walls.

I wanted to smash the box to let them out
but for fear of them I could not.

That frantic din grew faint. The day
we buried him his bees were still.

Sarah Brown Weitzman

HIS BEST

Nearly midnight when the bell rang
my mother and I weren't asleep
and opened the door for the man,
who was "Here for the clothes."

We went upstairs to fetch them.
We chose his best Sunday navy serge
and his best striped silk tie, and
a starched white folded shirt, his best.

I picked out dark blue socks
from scores of packs, tight as angry
fists, and a pair of shined leather shoes,
black, his best and nearly new.

The man took the suit, the tie
and the shirt, with bowed thanks.
"Don't need the socks or the shoes.
Feet don't show in a coffin."

Jess Witkins

THE FUNERAL PHOTOGRAPHER

I never thought I'd be asked to play photographer at a funeral. Especially when it was for my own brother-in-law.

"Should I smile or not smile?" my sister asked me. "I don't know what to do."

I held up my iPhone to focus the image.

She'd been crying again. In her arms, she held their youngest, just eight months old, a tuft of red hair sticking up from her otherwise bald head. And clinging to her side, was their oldest child, five, looking unsure and a little scared. Our family was never this quiet. The silence unnerved me too.

Behind them was the casket, half open, where my brother-in-law's body was laid out in a suit and tie.

I couldn't stare at Brian too long, it was upsetting. I looked instead at the brightly colored floral spree, full of purple and orange flowers – a combination Brian always liked together - resting on the casket's closed wooden end.

My sister asked me the night before.

"I can't decide if I want pictures of him in his casket or not."

I was sitting at the top of the stairs inside my parents' house, watching my sister apply makeup in the bathroom, trying to conceal the dark circles under her tired, weary eyes.

"On the one hand, I want the girls to be able to see someday, if they want to, that they were at the funeral. They're so young, they may not remember. I don't want them to feel they were left out," she said. "And on the other hand, it's creepy."

She had valid points both. Death is an unfamiliar, intimidating thing.

"We'll just play it by ear," I said. "Let me know tomorrow when we're there."

"Well, whatever you do, take them right away. I don't want his brother's wife to see you. She'll be totally freaked out."

"Got it."

I helped my sister write the eulogy. I'd never written a eulogy before. We sat at our parents' kitchen table, me with my laptop and my sister with a piece of scratch paper covered in pen on both sides. She'd been up most of the night scribbling every memory of Brian as they came to her. He was only 46. She was 37. They'd been together since she was 18.

My sister had written down stories of Brian as a little boy. The ones shared over and over at holidays. She wrote about what a family man he was, about the infamous time he caught a baseball at a Brewers game and gave it to his nephew. How he had nicknamed their youngest daughter, who at eight months would have no memory of his voice saying the words.

I wasn't sure I could cry at the funeral. I did, of course. The tears ambushed their way out. But I felt like someone needed to hold it together. Hold *us* together. My elegant sister stood in a trance, doing her duty as a young, grieving widow.

I was the funeral photographer that day. My lens showed the photo boards meticulously assembled to display only the happiest of times in a person's life. Like a movie. Like a Hollywood montage of great memories, one after the other. It should have worked out that way. Brian looked like a leading man.

My lens stood somewhere between the light over the casket and the darkness over the church pews. I captured the last time my sister would look at her husband's face. I captured the final kiss. The last time their family would be together, if together is what you can call it.

Ten days after the funeral, I made the familiar three hour drive down I-90. This time for my wedding. We didn't have programs or planned speeches, but what did they matter anyway?

As I drove to the wedding venue, alone in the car, I passed by the cemetery where Brian is buried, and I waved. I said all the things I needed to say to him. I told him I loved and missed him. I still do.

I took the photos my sister asked for. I hold them still, on standby. Until needed. If needed. I remain the witness of her grief. I captured three faces of loss in their last moment as a family. Their eyes were the eyes of sadness, uncertainty, and heartache. It was Brian's face, when I was able to look at it, that held the most peace.

◆◆◆

P.F. Witte

DEATH, BE AS PROUD AS YOU WANT

My father was not a man of "wants," seldom asking for anything for himself; maybe some new work clothes or work shoes, but that was more of a need. He was never known to wake up one morning and suddenly announce to the family that he wanted to buy a new car or a new house; he was fine with what he had, no more, no less.

It was only as my father approached retirement that he finally had something in his life he definitely wanted, and that was to be cremated when he died. The want became a demand when my mother, on hearing his request, could not understand why anyone in their right mind would want to be reduced to a heap of ashes.

"*Cremation?* What do I tell the neighbors? That the jar sitting on the top of the TV is my husband? *I* have to *live* with that?" My mother looked at my father with horror and disgust, as if he had already turned to ashes right in front of her. But the more horror she expressed at the very thought of it, the more my father insisted on being cremated.

For my father it was a no muss, no fuss deal—quick, easy, efficient, and cheap. He tried to reason with her; didn't my mother want to save money? And just as quickly she reasoned back--no, she didn't--just as she didn't want to save his ashes in their house for the rest of her living life.

My mother had always wanted to be married to a man who wore deep blue suits, white shirts, and ties; my father did when they first dated. But later on in married life when my father took a job as a truckdriver, the blue suits never came

124

out of the closet. My mother accepted that, got used to it, but cremation—never. My father had gone beyond the limits of all that was decent. Something had to be done, and my mother was never one to be defeated.

One day, after coming home from an afternoon of shopping, my mother had some great news for my father. She had just happened to be driving by Pinelawn (a bit out of her way since she did all her shopping in Queens, and Pinelawn was out on Long Island). "And guess what? There was a special going on. They gave me a good price on a plot, so I decided to buy two—one for you and one for me."

My father turned deep red with anger: "I told you, I'm not going to be buried in the ground, I'm going to be cremated. What the hell am I going to do way out at Pinelawn?" So there my mother stood with the certificates of purchase in hand.

I had just happened to stop by that afternoon for a visit, and walking through the door, my mother greeted me by flashing the certificates in my face, as if she had the winning numbers to the lottery, making me an offer she was sure I wouldn't refuse: "A plot, already paid for, Pinelawn, you'll never have to worry about having a place to rest, what do you say?" I looked at my mother as if she had lost her mind: "I'd say I'm not ready to die yet."

From that day on my mother never made mention of the plots again. My father would talk on occasion about the benefits of cremation to anyone at home who would listen, and if my mother happened to be around she would simply shake her head, make an excuse that the coffee pot needed cleaning, and remove herself to the kitchen. That's the way it remained until my father's death.

Talk about cremation resurfaced when my father wound up in the hospital some eleven years later, and was diagnosed with emphysema—he was now a dying man with one wish—cremation. Then again, my mother was a woman who was still very much alive, with one wish also, *and* with two plots on her hands. What to do?

The burial. We stand before the freshly dug six-foot plot, my mother, my sister, and me. The man at the foot of the grave who is reciting from the bible looks exactly like Frankenstein—this is no exaggeration—he is part of another "special deal" my mother purchased through the funeral home in Queens. He stands six-foot-seven and rail-thin to the bone, has a great shock of black hair, wears an ill-fitted black suit from which his pale white wrists are noticeably exposed, and pant legs that barely reach the ankles—that's how I notice his clubbed foot (one of his shoes has at least a six-inch rubber platform to compensate for one leg being shorter than the other). He wears thin wire-rimmed glasses, and it is only because he is reading from the bible that he appears to be a kinder, gentler Frankenstein.

Finally, he recites the line "ashes to ashes and dust to dust," and a small cardboard box, no more than a foot long and a foot wide, is carefully lowered into the six-foot grave. mother nudges me and whispers, "The urn with your father's ashes is inside the box." And then as an afterthought, nudges me and whispers again, "It was a great price on a plot, I couldn't let it just sit there empty."

◆ ◆ ◆

Editor's Note

Anecdotally, at least, it is becoming more common for people surveying the lives they have led and contemplating the end to take the matter of the obituary into their own hands. In recent years, some of these have become popular on the internet, particularly when they exhibit a measure of biting political humor or a no-holds-barred account of a colorful life.

Others, however, are intended not to settle scores or make a partisan statement, but rather to strive for a balanced and nuanced accounting of one person's time on Earth."Grácias a La Vida Que Me Ha Dado Tanto" is one of those. In it, the writer looks back on a long and rich life and homes in on the people and things that have made it so.

---

*(Song lyrics by Violeta Parra Sandoval, sung by Mercedes Sosa of Argentina. Scan this QR Code to listen to ."Grácias a La Vida Que Me Ha Dado Tanto" here:

Anonymous

GRACIAS A LA VIDA QUE ME HA DADO TANTO*
(Thanks to the Life that Has Given Me So Much)

A personal farewell:
I was born in Salem, Oregon, resisted growing up in Albany, Oregon, and obtained a BA at the University of Oregon.

The greatest gifts I have received in my life have been my wife and our daughter. They followed me and gave me unconditional love wherever my adventures took them.

My father was a man who taught me not to be too judgmental and to accept people on their own terms. My mother was always curious about the world that, sadly only after her early death, her eldest son explored. I have two stalwart brothers who live in Oregon. They are honorable men whom I love and respect. We three were always very different from each other. Tom was a senior officer in the Oregon State Police and Doug a corporate financial officer and CPA.

In the beginning of my adulthood, I flunked out of college, lost an athletic scholarship and joined the US Army where I was trained as a German linguist and sent to Germany. My commanders arranged for me to work night shifts so I could attend a semester at the nearby Friedrich Alexander Universitaet in Erlangen, Germany. Thus began a long adventure that after completing graduate school in Arizona led me to travel to more than 85 countries and over thirty years residence in six lands other than my native United States.

My career was always concerned with the wheat industry, managing flour mills in Venezuela and Colombia, and working for a contractor with the US Department of Agriculture developing export markets for American wheat while living in the Netherlands and, later, Chile. During my years in the Netherlands, I opened corporate operations in the Soviet Union and the European Satellite states. In later years I became the founding Director of the California Wheat Commission and afterward headed the Wheat Marketing Center in Portland, Oregon, where we studied the technologies and raw materials requirements associated with the unique wheat-based products of Asia.

For five years after my retirement and until I moved to Mexico I traveled extensively as a consultant in the Middle East, North Africa and Asia and served as an advisor to technical schools in Venezuela, Egypt and Morocco.

Many times, I have been asked which was my favorite place to live. I have always answered that I have loved every place I have lived or visited for the uniqueness and idiosyncrasies of their cultures and the beauty of their landscape and architecture. I have had welcoming friends and associates across the spectrum of the places I have been.

My retirement in Ajijic, Jalisco, Mexico, in 2005 has brought me a new career as a novelist and short story writer and has enclosed me in a circle of the deepest and most enduring friendships of my life. My books are on amazon.com and short stories appear in my website.

Yes indeed, *Grácias a la vida que me ha dado tanto.*
Adios.

◆ ◆ ◆

Notes on Contributors

Virginia Barrett's books of poetry include *Between Looking*, Finishing Line Press (2019) *Crossing Haight*, and I *Just Wear My Wings*. Barrett is the editor of two anthologies of contemporary San Francisco poets including *OCCUPY SF— poems from the movement*. Her work has most recently appeared in the *Writer's Chronicle, Narrative, Roar: Literature and Revolution by Feminist People, Ekphrastic Review, Weaving the Terrain* (Dos Gatos Press), and *Poetry of Resistance: Voices for Social Justice* (University of Arizona Press). She received a 2017 writer's residency grant from the Helene Wurlitzer Foundation of Taos, NM. She has been nominated for a Pushcart Prize.

Sidney Bending is a retired graphic artist living on the west coast of Canada. Her award-winning poems have been published in literary journals and anthologies in North America, Europe, and New Zealand. Her chapbook of small poems is available from leafpress.ca In 2017 she co-edited a book of haiku/senryu called this tiny shell. Sidney is a member of Haiku Canada, the Haiku Society of America, and the British Haiku Society.

Hannah Bleier teaches children to read in Boston. She has been failing to write a great poem, story, or essay since the age of eleven, but she keeps trying.

Nancy Brewka-Clark's poems appear in many publications including *The North American Review*, *Visiting Frost: Poems Inspired by the Life and Work of Robert Frost* from The University of Iowa Press, *Beloved on the Earth* by Holy Cow! Press, and *Two-Countries* from Red Hen Press, which received the 2018 bronze medal in the Multicultural Non-Fiction Adult category. She is a previous winner of the Helen Schaible International Sonnet Competition and was a finalist in the international Thomas Merton Poetry of the Sacred competition.

Laurie Byro has had five collections of poetry published, most recently *La Dogaressa* (Cowboy Buddha Press). Two collections had work that received a New Jersey Poetry Prize. Her poetry has received 54 Interboard Competition honors including 10 First Place awards as judged. In 2018, she was nominated for four Pushcart Prizes and she facilitates Circle of Voices in NJ Libraries for the last 18 years.

Dane Cervine's books include *Kung Fu of the Dark Father (2015), How Therapists Dance (2013),* and, *The Jeweled Net of Indra (2007).* Saddle Road Press will publish his new cross-genre work of Zen koan & prose poems in 2018, entitled *The Gateless Gate – Polishing the Moon Sword.* Dane's poems have won awards from Adrienne Rich, Tony Hoagland, the *Atlanta Review, Caesura,* and been nominated for a Pushcart. His work appears in *The SUN, the Hudson Review, TriQuarterly, Poetry Flash, Catamaran, Miramar, Rattle, Sycamore Review, Pedestal Magazine,* among others.

Visit his website at: www.DaneCervine.typepad.com

Lucia Cherciu was born in Romania and came to the United States in 1995. She is a Professor of English at SUNY / Dutchess in Poughkeepsie, NY and writes both in English and in Romanian. She is the author of two books of poetry in English: *Train Ride to Bucharest* (Sheep Meadow Press, 2017), which was the winner of the Eugene Paul Nassar Poetry Prize, and *Edible Flowers* (Main Street Rag, 2015), and three books in Romanian: *Lalele din Paradis / Tulips in Paradise* (Editura Eikon, 2017), *Altoiul Râsului / Grafted Laughter* (Editura Brumar, 2010), and *Lepădarea de Limbă / The Abandonment of Language* (Editura Vinea, 2009).
Her work was nominated three times for a Pushcart Prize and twice for Best of the Net. Her web page is http://luciacherciu.webs.com.

Marc Alan Di Martino's poems have been published in *Rattle, Poets Reading the News, Poetry Salzburg Review* and other places. He lives in Italy, where he teaches English as a foreign language.

J.C. Elkin is an essayist and poet whose prize-winning work has appeared in such publications as *Kestrel, Angle, The Delmarva Review,* and *Steam Ticket.* She has lived from coast to coast and in Europe – always singing and learning new languages.
Her chapbook *World Class: Poems Inspired by the ESL Classroom* (Apprentice House, 2014) is based on her experiences teaching English to Adults from around the world. She holds an MFA from Bennington Writing Seminars.

A native Californian, **Meredith Escudier** has lived in France for over 35 years, teaching, translating and raising a family. She is the author of three books: *Scene in France, Frenchisms for Francophiles* and most recently a food memoir, *The Taste of Forever,* an affectionate examination of home cooks that features an American mother and a French husband.

Beverly Butler Faragasso's husband has Parkinson's Disease. Living with his illness causes them to think about, worry about, their own mortality. Will one more hospital stay be their last? Because of this uneasy push-pull between life and death, "what remains" intrigued Butler Faragasso. Her grandmother's funeral program reminded her that, in the end, what will matter, what will remain, will be sweet, precious memories. Butler Faragasso is a retired college professor.

Jeanne Finley is a photographer, writer, and editor in Albany, New York. Her poetry, short fiction, and non-fiction have been published in literary magazines and journals, and her photographs have been exhibited in galleries and other venues in and around the Capital District. She is also a community activist for social justice. Her photography website is www.jeannefinley.com

Nina Gaby is a writer, visual artist, and advanced practice nurse who specializes in addiction and psychiatry. Her essays, fiction, prose poetry, and articles have been published in anthologies and magazines, and her artwork is held in various collections, including the Smithsonian's. In addition to a master's degree in psych-mental health nursing, Gaby holds bachelor's degrees in fine arts and nursing and has taught at several universities.

Elaine Garrett is a K-12 science outreach coordinator in Upstate New York . This is her first anthology contribution. She holds a BFA in Film, Photography, and Visual Arts, and an MA in Museum Education.

After years of working as a Senior Acquisitions Editor in major New York publishing houses, **Sandi Gelles-Cole** realized that editors were being moved further from the editing process—the hands-on work with the written word that was her passion. In 1983 she left the corporate setting and became an independent editor. She works with commercial fiction and non-fiction and functions as a developmental, structural, and/or line editor, depending on what the project requires. Three-quarters of her projects are fiction, and these tend to be aimed at women readers, though not genre fiction. For non-fiction, the titles that best define me are women's role in business; women's psychological and physical health; works on relationships, and memoirs, especially those of affliction, family dysfunction or violence against women; true crime. Gelles-Cole Literary Enterprises is also the publisher of several small press titles. For additional information and a look at some of the titles she has edited, see literaryenterprises.com.

Linda G. Kaplan is happily retired from New York State Service as a Legal Affairs Specialist. She began writing as a way to express her pain in watching her father's descent into Parkinson's Disease when he lost his mobility and speech. She attended the summer workshops held at Skidmore College in Saratoga Springs, NY offered by the International Women's Writing Guild and joined a local offshoot called WomanWords organized by Marilyn Day. She has read her poetry at the Cafe Lena and various local venues and recorded one of her essays that was broadcast on NPR. She also became a potter and enjoys playing with clay. Linda is happily married and lives in Guilderland, New York.

Paul Hostovsky is the author of nine books of poetry, most recently, *Is That What That Is* (FutureCycle Press, 2017). He has won a Pushcart Prize, two Best of the Net awards, and has been featured on *Poetry Daily*, *Verse Daily*, and *The Writer's Almanac*. He makes his living in Boston as an ASL interpreter and Braille instructor. To read more of his work, visit him at www.paulhostovsky.com

Ronn Kilby wasted more than three decades working for television stations around the country as art director, writer/producer and senior creative director. He currently produces commercials, documentaries and narrative films on a freelance basis. His latest project is *SKIN: The Movie*, a comedy "with a heart" was released in winter 2018. Ronn enjoys woodworking, motorcycle touring and spoiling his nine above average grandchildren. He lives in San Diego with his very patient bride, Marti.

Peggy Landsman is the author of a poetry chapbook, *To-wit To-woo* (Foothills Publishing). Her work has been published or is forthcoming in many literary journals and anthologies, including *The Muse Strikes Back* (Story Line Press), *Breathe: 101 Contemporary Odes* (C&R Press), and, most recently, *Nasty Women Poets: An Unapologetic Anthology Of Subversive Verse* (Lost Horse Press), *SWWIM Every Day*, and *Mezzo Cammin*.
She currently lives in South Florida where she swims in the warm Atlantic Ocean every chance she gets.

https://peggylandsman.wordpress.com/

John Laue is a teacher/counselor and a former editor of *Transfer* and Associate Editor of *San Francisco Review*. He has won awards for his writing and is the author of five published chapbooks and a book of prose advice for people diagnosed as mentally ill. He coordinates the reading series of the Monterey Bay Poetry Consortium, and edits the online magazine *Monterey Poetry Review*. His full-length book of dramatic poems, *A Confluence of Voices*, is published by Futurecycle Press.

Tina Lincer, a native of Queens, N.Y., is a writer and painter. Her essays and op-eds have appeared in The *New York Daily News*, Albany *Times Union, The Sun, Writer's Digest, and authormagazine.com,* as well as on public radio. Her essays also are featured in numerous anthologies, including *Words on Ice* (Key Porter Books) and *Living Apart Together* (Friesen Press). She lives in upstate New York and is at work on a memoir and a novel.

Claire Loader was born in New Zealand and spent several years in China before moving to County Galway, Ireland, where she now lives with her family. A photographer and writer, she was a recent finalist in the *Women Speak* poetry competition and blogs at www.allthefallingstones.com. Her work has appeared in various publications, including *Crannóg, Dodging The Rain* and *Pendora.*

Fran Markover lives in Ithaca, NY, where she works as psychotherapist. Her poems have been published in journals including *Rattle, Calyx, Sow's Ear Poetry Review, Karamu, Runes,*

Spillway, Earth's Daughters, Able Muse. Recent awards include a poetry residency at the Constance Saltonstall Foundation for the Arts and a Pushcart Prize nomination. Her chapbook *History's Trail,* was published by Finishing Line Press.

Kerry Dean Martinez spent many years moving all over the place. Former waitress, cook on a sport fishing boat, teacher, program manager, doctoral dropout, executive director, and finally helping Mr. Joe Martinez with his businesses, including the Golden Hours Lounge, of blessed memory. She lives mostly in Portugal these days.

José Miramontes is a husband, father, and businessman in Ajijic, Mexico, on the shores of Lake Chapala. This is his first appearance in print.

Sheryl L. Nelms is from the Flint Hills of Kansas. She graduated from South Dakota State University. She's had over 5,000 articles, stories and poems published, including eighteen individual collections of her poems*. She's the fiction/nonfiction editor of *The Pen Woman Magazine*, the National League of American Pen Women publication and a four time Pushcart Prize nominee.*Extensive credits listing @ Sheryl L. Nelms at www.pw.org/directory/featured

Bonnie Neubauer is the author of motivational writing books: *The Write-Brain Workbook Revised & Expanded: 400 Exercises to Liberate Your Writing* (Writer's Digest Books); *303 Writing Prompts: Ideas to Get You Started* (Fall River Press/Sterling Publishing); and *Take Ten for Writers: 1,000 Inspiring Exercises* (Writer's Digest Books). She is also the inventor of *Story Spinner,* a handheld and digital tool for generating millions of creative writing exercises. Bonnie runs fun and funny writing workshops for all ages and levels.

Opeyemi Parham practiced family medicine for just over twenty years as Dr. Camilla Parham. Eleven years "post-doctoring," she believes that those initials behind her name signify "Feral Physician (once domesticated, but returned to the WILD) and Mistress of Death" (having learned mightily from her own Near Death Experience). As a writer she has an essay in *Hope Beneath Our Feet* and a chapter in *Dancing on the Earth: Women's Stories of Healing, Through Dance*. She can be found on Facebook at *The Temple of The Healthy Spirit*, or at her website, www.ceremonyheals.com.

A native New Yorker, **James Penha** lives in Indonesia. Nominated for Pushcart Prizes in fiction and poetry, his story "By the Banyan Tree" appears in the 2018 Lambda Literary Award winning anthology *His Seed* while his dystopian poem "2020" is part of the 2017 *Not My President* collection. His essay "It's Been a Long Time Coming" was featured in *The New York Times* "Modern Love" column in April 2016. Penha edits *TheNewVerse.News*, an online journal of current-events poetry.

Herbert W. Piekow was born during the Second World War to a Jewish father and a French speaking mother. He has worked in Pakistan and later was a part of the transformation of the Kingdom of Saudi Arabia into the twenty-first century. His writing career began in the seventh grade. He has written for magazines, newspapers and been a columnist and content editor for monthly publications both in the United States and in Mexico, where he lives. He has won awards for news, content, style and writing.

Holly Pruett is a Life-Cycle Celebrant, Home Funeral Guide, and co-creator of Oregon Funeral Resources & Education, a public interest website (OregonFuneral.org). A well-known conversation leader and consultant, Holly founded PDX Death Café and the Death Talk Project, and facilitated with Oregon Humanities' Talking about Dying Conversation Program. She has a Masters Degree in Applied Behavioral Science, studies with Stephen Jenkinson's Orphan Wisdom School, and is certified in Thanatology by the Association for Death Education & Counseling.

Tony Reevy's previous publications include poetry, non-fiction and short fiction, including the non-fiction books *Ghost Train!, O. Winston Link: Life Along the Line* and *The Railroad Photography of Jack Delano*, the poetry chapbooks *Green Cove Stop, Magdalena, Lightning in Wartime,* and *In Mountain Lion Country,* and the full books of poetry, *Old North, Passage* and *Socorro.* He resides in Durham, North Carolina with wife, Caroline Weaver, and children Lindley and Ian.

Carlos Reyes is a widely published poet and translator. He is the author of 10 volumes of Poetry and many volumes of translations. Latest poetry: *Guilt in Our Pockets, Poems from South India* (2017), *Along the Flaggy Shore, Poems from West Clare* (2018). Most recent book of translations: *Poems of Love and Madness, Poemas de amor y locura* (2013). He is also the author of a prose memoir, *The Keys to the Cottage , Stories from the West of Ireland* (2015). He has been awarded a Heinrich Boll

Fellowship (Achill, Ireland) and has been a Yaddo Fellow (New York).

Natalie Safir is the author of *Eyewitness* (Dos Madres Press, 2016), her sixth book of poetry. Her poems have appeared in many literary journals and have been anthologized in *Art & Artists* (Penguin Everyman edition) and *A Slant of Light*, among others.

She has taught Memoir and Creative Fiction and had essays published in *Child of My Child*, *Persimmon Tree*, and an essay with fairytale in *The Fairygodmentor's Advice* (Indiana Purdue University Press).

Kenneth Salzmann's poetry has appeared in such journals and magazines as *Chiron Review, Monthly Review, Rattle, Comstock Review, Stockholm Literary Review*, and many more, and is collected in such anthologies as *Beloved on the Earth: 150 Poems of Grief and Gratitude, Riverine: An Anthology of Hudson Valley Writers, Child of My Child*, and others. He currently lives in Central Mexico.

Gerard Sarnat MD has been nominated for Pushcarts and won other prizes. *Kaddish for the Country* was selected for pamphlet distribution on Inauguration Day nationwide. Amber Of Memory was the single poem chosen for his 50th Harvard reunion Dylan symposium; The *Harvard Advocate* accepted a second.

Gerard is a physician who has built/staffed homeless clinics, a Stanford professor/healthcare CEO. Collections: *Homeless Chronicles* (2010), *Disputes, 17s, Melting the Ice King* (2016). Married since 1969; he has seven grand/kids. www.gerardsarnat.com.

Mary Ann Savage is a native of West Virginia. She earned aher M.S. degree in Clinical Psychology from the University of Pittsburgh, and now lives and writes in Watsonville, California.

Patti See's work has appeared in *Salon Magazine, Women's Studies Quarterly, The Wisconsin Academy Review, The Southwest Review, HipMama, Inside HigherEd,* as well as many other magazines and anthologies. She is the co-editor (with Bruce Taylor) of *Higher Learning: Reading and Writing About College,* 3rd edition (Pearson/Prentice Hall, 2011) and a poetry collection, *Love's Bluff* (Plainview Press, 2006). Her blog "Our Long Goodbye: One Family's Experiences with Alzheimer's" has been read in over 100 countries.

Linda Simone is the author of *Archeology* and *Cow* Tippers, and the forthcoming collection *The River Will Save Us* (Aldrich Press/Kelsay Books). Her Pushcart-nominated poems appear in numerous journals and anthologies. Her essay, "The Stubborn Poem: Tackle or Trash?" is forthcoming in the anthology *Far Villages: Welcome Essays for New and Beginner Poets* (Black Lawrence Press). A native New Yorker, she now lives in San Antonio, Texas. http://www.lindasimone.com/

Richelle Lee Slota travels frequently from her home in San Francisco to visit her family in Nigeria and West Africa. She writes plays, novels, nonfiction and poetry. She and her co-author, Yaw Boateng, just published, on Amazon, a piece of investigative journalism: Captive Market: Commercial Kidnapping Stories from Nigeria. Her short play, We All Walk In Shoes Too Small was produced at the Royal Academy of Dramatic Art, London. *Dream Big* and *Famous*

Michael were staged by Solano Repertory Company in Northern California. She is a Vietnam era vet. She earned BA's in Psychology and Theatre Arts and an MA in Creative Writing. She has three grown children and is a member of the Playwright's Center of San Francisco.

Joseph Stanton is a Professor of Art History and American Studies at the University of Hawai'i at Mānoa and a widely published poet. His poems have appeared in *Poetry, Poetry East, Harvard Review, Ekphrasis, New York Quarterly*, and many other journals and anthologies.

Alison Stone's books are *Dazzle* (Jacar Press, 2018), *Masterplan*, with Eric Greinke (Presa Press, 2018), *Ordinary Magic*, (NYQ Books, 2016), *Dangerous Enough* (Presa Press 2014), and *They Sing at Midnight*, which won the Many Mountains Moving Poetry Award. Her poems have appeared in *The Paris Review, Poetry, Ploughshares*, and other journals. She was awarded *Poetry*'s Frederick Bock Prize and *New York Quarterly*'s Madeline Sadin Award. She is a painter and created The Stone Tarot. www.stonepoetry.org

A high school English teacher, **Katherine Barrett Swett** lives in New York City. She received a PhD in American Literature from Columbia University.
Her poems have been published in various journals including, *The Lyric, Rattle, Mezzo Cammin, The Raintown Review* and *Measure*. Her chapbook, *Twenty-one* was published by Finishing Line Press in 2016.
Her collection, *Voice Message* was selected by Erica Dawson for the 2019 Donald Justice Poetry Prize. It will be published by Autumn House Press in 2020.

Margaret Van Every was born and raised in St. Louis, Missouri, but lived most of her life in Tallahassee, Florida. For many years she was a professional writer-editor and instructional developer. In retirement she moved to the mountains of Mexico where she currently pursues her passions of writing and chamber music.

She is the author of *A Pillow Stuffed with Diamonds* (Librophilia 2010); *A Pillow Stuffed with Diamonds Bilingual* (Librophilia 2011); *Saying Her Name* (Librophilia 2013); and *holding hands with a stranger* (Librophilia 2014).

She also writes short stories and essays and is a frequent contributor to the Mexican journal *El Ojo del Lago*. Her poems and stories appear in numerous anthologies, and in 2018 she edited and published the final collection of poetry by James Tipton, *The Alphabet of Longing and Other Poems* (Librophilia).

Sandy Warren is a freelance writer specializing in writing about food and cooking, as well as interviews with musicians. Based in Atlantic City, New Jersey, she is the author of *Art Blakey Cookin' and Jammin': Recipes and Remembrances from a Jazz Life*, a culinary memoir of her relationship with the legendary jazz drummer, and was producer and co-writer of the documentary film, *Horn From the Heart: The Paul Butterfield Story*.

Sarah Brown Weitzman, a past National Endowment for the Arts Fellow in Poetry and Pushcart Prize nominee, has had poems published in hundreds of journals and anthologies, including *The New Ohio Review*, *The North American Review*, *The Bellingham Review*, *Rattle*, *Mid-American*

Review, Poet Lore, Miramar, and elsewhere. Pudding House published her chapbook, *The Forbidden.*

Jess Witkins is a writer, blogger, and storyteller in western Wisconsin. She's a member of the nonprofit writing community, Women Writers Ink, and has been a director, producer, and performer in the national series, *Listen To Your Mother.*

P.F. Witte is a New York City writer. She has won the Pat Parker Memorial Poetry Award and the Allen Ginsberg Poetry Series Award among others. Her fiction and non-fiction work has appeared in the anthologies: *The Muse Strikes Back, Women on the Verge, The Writer's Place, and The Literary Journal of the Kurt Vonnegut Museum and Library.* She has given extensive readings, among them: Columbia University, Barnes & Noble Bookstores, La Mama Theater, and The AIDS Theater Project.

ACKNOWLEDGMENTS

Some works included in *What Remains* originally appeared the following publications:

Southeast Lighthouse Stairs, Block Island by Laurie Byro was included in her book, *Luna*.

On Mentioning That Our Daughter Wants to Be A Mortician by Nina Gaby first appeared in *Dodge Magazine*.

City of Refuge by Katherine Barrett Swett was originally published in *Rattle*.

The Persistence of Ashes by Kenneth Salzmann was first published in *Riverine: An Anthology of Hudson Valley Writers*.

Also available from Gelles-Cole Literary Enterprises

Child of My Child: Poems and Stories for Grandparents

The Memoir of Marilyn Monroe by Sandi Gelles-Cole

The Last Jazz Fan and Other Poems by Kenneth Salzmann

Coming in 2020: *What But the Music: Baby Boomers Write About the Soundtrack of Their Lives*

All titles available from Gelles-Cole Literary Enterprises

CPSIA information can be obtained
at www.ICGtesting.com
Printed in the USA
BVHW041814010421
603947BV00015B/655